U

Please

Cla
...

Purchasing Contracts:
A PRACTICAL GUIDE

CHANDOS BUSINESS GUIDES
PROCUREMENT AND PURCHASING

Chandos Business Guides are designed to provide managers with practical, down-to-earth information. The Chandos Business Guides are written by leading authors in their respective fields. If you would like to receive a full listing of current and forthcoming titles, please visit our web site www.chandospublishing.com or contact Melinda Taylor on email mtaylor@chandospublishing.com or direct telephone number +44 (0) 1865 882727.

New authors: we are always pleased to receive ideas for new titles; if you would like to write a Chandos Business Guide, please contact Dr Glyn Jones on email gjones@chandospublishing.com or direct telephone number +44 (0) 1865 884447.

Bulk orders: some organisations buy a number of copies of our books. If you are interested in doing this, we would be pleased to discuss a discount. Please contact Dr Glyn Jones on email gjones@chandospublishing.com or direct telephone number +44 (0) 1865 884447.

PURCHASING CONTRACTS:
A PRACTICAL GUIDE

GRAHAM FULLER

Chandos Publishing

Oxford · England

Chandos Publishing (Oxford) Limited
Chandos House
5 & 6 Steadys Lane
Stanton Harcourt
Oxford OX8 1RL
England
Tel: +44 (0) 1865 882727 Fax: +44 (0) 1865 884448
Email: sales@chandospublishing.com
www.chandospublishing.com

• •

First published in Great Britain in 2001

ISBN 1 902375 71 8

© G. Fuller, 2001

Typeset by Turn-Around Typesetting
Printed by Biddles, Guildford, UK

Contents

Preface

This book is not intended to be a comprehensive study of the law of contract. There are a number of excellent books performing this function and the reader who, for examination purposes or otherwise, requires an in-depth knowledge of the subject should refer to them.

The aim has been to focus on those areas of the law which time has led me to believe are of the greatest concern for those whose work is with contracts for the procurement of goods and services. Accordingly, some areas of contract law, including the doctrines of misrepresentation and mistake, have been afforded only passing mention or no mention at all. I have provided more detail on topics which are the subject of recent legislation where it is expected the reader will be looking for guidance.

In addition to principles of contract law, other matters are dealt with, including drafting techniques, the problems of electronic contracting and the ethical aspects of the purchasing process.

In earlier times a book of this kind would have been called a *vade mecum* – a compact manual intended to serve as a friendly companion. Quite commonly, the user of such a volume would supplement it by the addition of handwritten notes recording his or her own experiences and comments. If this book comes to be regarded as a well-meaning friend to its owner then I will be delighted.

Acknowledgements

I would like to express my gratitude to Mr Kenneth Burnett of the Chartered Institute of Purchasing & Supply and to Professor Geoffrey Woodroffe for their valuable suggestions and advice. I, alone, bear full responsibility for any defects in quality.

The generosity of Mrs Elizabeth Balmer and Mr John Mackenzie in reading the script and the kindness of the staff of the Law Library of Bristol University are also much appreciated.

My deepest debt is to Jarmila, my wife and sternest critic, who has devoted her time and skill to this project with not only her characteristic energy and kindness but with uncharacteristic patience.

Table of cases

Table of statutes

PURCHASING CONTRACTS: A PRACTICAL GUIDE

The author

Graham Fuller is a visiting lecturer on purchasing matters at Warwick University, School of Engineering and Management, a regular lecturer for the Institute of Purchasing and Supply and presenter of its Law for the Buyer and Contract Drafting conferences. As a graduate in Law he was called to the bar in 1969 and practised until 1976 when he took up the position of Senior Crown Counsel to the Hong Kong government. Until 1998 he was Senior Legal Adviser to Rolls-Royce plc, advising on matters including international joint ventures, technology transfers and purchase contracts.

The author may be contacted via the publishers.

CHAPTER 1

Written contracts and the purchaser

Most contracts are made orally or by conduct. We buy our newspapers, petrol and food without feeling the slightest need for a document. When the window cleaner comes we don't ask him to sign a contract. Deals like these are so simple because the agreement and performance of them closely follow one another and the risk of things going wrong is low – there is just no need for a written contract.

And even if things do go wrong we are able to claim for a breach of a term implied by the appropriate statute. If, for example, the window cleaner puts his ladder through a window he will be in breach of the term implied by statute into contracts for services that he will carry out the service with reasonable care and skill.

The professional purchaser lives in a very different world because commercial contracts are often:

- more complex;

- take longer to perform; and

- may cause the purchaser serious loss if, for example, delivery is late.

Moreover, where the purchaser is not a person but a company, local authority or similar, it is dependent upon human agents to make its contracts for it. It will not help much if an employee has entered an oral contract and by the time things have started to go wrong is found to have emigrated, cannot be contacted or cannot remember a thing about it.

A written agreement gives three benefits:

- the best evidence that the parties have reached a binding agreement rather than that they have merely had discussions;

- the opportunity to set out clearly the respective rights and duties of the parties; and

- the chance to review it before finalising it and to reflect on the wisdom of entering the particular transaction.

The first is self-explanatory. The second may be illustrated by the following example:

> A purchase manager buys a sophisticated machine tool. When it is delivered his technical colleagues will need to make a detailed examination of it to ensure it complies with contract

specification. If it does not, they will want to reject it. They – and the purchase manager – are aware that the law only allows a limited period before this right of rejection is lost.

Without a written contract it is necessary to rely upon the term implied by section 35 of the Sale of Goods Act 1979 (see Chapter 7) which gives the purchaser *a reasonable opportunity* to ascertain whether the goods correspond with their description. When asked how long this period is, it will be impossible to give a precise answer; what is *reasonable* will depend upon the inference a particular judge draws from the facts of the case.

Of course, an oral agreement with the supplier could have included express agreement of a finite inspection period, but then we are back to the matter of proof; employees do tend to adjust their memories to help their employers and to keep themselves out of trouble!

In these circumstances it is much better to have a clear written contract which includes a clause as follows:

> The purchaser may, within seven weeks from delivery, reject the machine if it does not comply with its contract specification.

The third benefit is also important. When there is a written draft which is nearing completion then the terms of the deal are readily apparent from it. It also allows copies to be given to colleagues for their comments. If this is done they cannot say later that they were not informed as to what was going on!

A well-known saying in purchase departments is: 'When we make a purchase contract it goes in the drawer and then we all forget about it.' Regrettably, the implication of such a remark is that the whole process of drafting, agreeing and executing contracts is a waste of time. It is quite true that if everything runs smoothly there will be little need to pore over the paperwork, but life is often not that simple. Suppliers *do* deliver late and *do* provide defective goods and services. When things go wrong it is the contract which should serve as a clear guide to the extent of the supplier's liability.

The speaker may say, 'But we don't rush headlong into litigation. We sit down with the seller and sort things out. Litigation is the very last resort.' Quite right! But when both sides try to sort out the mess they need to have a pretty good idea of their contractual position. The proper way to negotiate a compromise is with a full understanding of the legal consequences for the purchaser and the supplier if they fail to reach a compromise and have to hand it over to the lawyers. To start *any* negotiation without an understanding of one's strengths and weaknesses is bad practice.

The written contract is there to tell both the purchaser and the supplier the rules under which they are to work together. The supplier particularly must understand that it has to follow those rules just as much as if both sides were playing a card game or a sport. Emphasis is placed on the need for *the supplier* to understand and comply with the contract as it is the supplier who has the majority of the contractual duties.

Beware of people who are dismissive of the purchase contract function. This attitude is often due to laziness – preparing good contracts requires a lot of mental discipline and hard work. Often these same people, with their private affairs, take any amount of care to make sure they get the best deal for themselves that they can!

If this assertion is doubted it may be interesting to test it by asking them what their holiday entitlement is or how much of it they have already used. They nearly always have a very clear idea of their own entitlements under their contracts of employment!

CHAPTER 2

Prior commitment

This chapter is particularly intended for purchasers of *long lead-time items* – where there is a sizeable gap between the time when the contract is made and the time when the supplier is able to deliver the goods. The time gap may be due to one or more of a number of factors: complexity of manufacture or the need to procure materials and components from many different sources. Although it is assumed the subject of the contract is goods, similar considerations apply to a contract for services – where the supplier needs, for example, to procure specialist equipment or to employ and train staff who will be able and ready to perform the contract.

The problem seems to come when the purchaser, for one reason or another, intends to sell the goods on to an end customer and that customer is unable or unwilling to enter into a contract with a lead-time as long as that required by the supplier. This reluctance may arise because the end customer is constrained from placing a firm order for budgetary or other reasons and has to say to the purchaser: 'I won't be able to enter into a firm commitment with you for another two months but if and when I do commit, I'll need delivery within two months.' If the purchaser has been told by its supplier that the lead-time is four months then something needs to be done.

The purchaser's ideal position is for the supplier to start work upon a *speculative basis* – that is, to start the procurement and manufacture of the goods prior to entering a contract. Not surprisingly (particularly with high value items and/or items which might be difficult for the supplier to sell elsewhere) the supplier will be reluctant to do so and will want contract cover. Here, the purchaser will need to use all its persuasive powers to get the supplier to take the risk and start work. The supplier will probably be told that he owes it to the purchaser as their relationship is a *partnership* (more will be said about that later) and that the supplier must take the chance if it wants the business.

Up to this point the purchaser is on safe ground. It is making it clear that it wants the supplier to start work upon the express basis that there may never be a contract and, hence, no payment for the supplier.

Sometimes, however, purchasers go further: they enter into some kind of intermediate agreement which is intended to make the supplier feel more secure but which the purchaser hopes, or believes, is not a legally enforceable contract. Such documents are often, rather coyly, called a *heads of agreement*, a *memorandum of understanding*, a *protocol* or a *letter of intent*.

One of the fundamental principles of English law is that the courts are not bedazzled by labels. If the true intention of the document is that the supplier should start work with the expectation of being paid then the supplier is entitled to be paid a reasonable price for its efforts.

Another highly dangerous practice is for the purchaser to tell a supplier that, although it is not possible to issue a purchase order straightaway, one will be sent at a future date. Sometimes the supplier is even given the serial number of the purchase order. Again, if the purchase order never comes, the chances are the supplier will be entitled to be paid a reasonable price for its work up to the time of cancellation.

What has been said so far is intended to stress that it is highly dangerous to try to lull a supplier into a false sense of security. If the supplier is to be on risk by procuring and manufacturing speculatively then this must be made clear.

If the supplier insists on contractual cover, what can be done to minimise the purchaser's liability if its end customer never does place a contract?

One useful approach is to try to agree a *termination for convenience* clause. The law of contract does not imply any right for a purchaser to change its mind and cancel a contract. In the absence of an express clause, if the purchaser makes it clear that it will not take delivery of the goods nor pay the purchase price, it has committed an *anticipatory breach* of contract.

It used to be thought that when this happened the supplier had a choice. It could carry on, complete the manufacturing, tender delivery on the due date and claim payment of the contract price. Alternatively, it could notify the purchaser it accepted the repudiation, stop work and claim for its loss of profit (the profit it would have made if the goods have been completed) plus all costs incurred, minus anything which could be salvaged by way of disposing of the item in its state of partial completion at the time of acceptance of the anticipatory breach.

Later cases have thrown doubt on the right of a supplier to ignore the breach. It has been suggested that the supplier, although the innocent party, must act reasonably and mitigate the damage. And so, for example, if cancellation by the purchaser takes place very early on a court might view the supplier as acting unreasonably if it continued with the contract and refuse to award it the greater amount.

An express *termination for convenience* clause avoids these problems. Such a clause usually provides that the purchaser:

- may terminate at any time before delivery;

- shall pay all costs incurred by the supplier up to the date of termination;

- shall be entitled to delivery of all work in progress or to require the supplier to dispose of it and deduct the proceeds from the costs; and

- shall be given a full account of the make-up of how the supplier has calculated its termination claim and have some rights of audit of the calculation.

Whether the clause should allow the supplier to claim anything for loss of profit, and if so, how much, is a matter for negotiation.

It is also wise to limit the supplier's recoverable costs to materials and components expended on the goods and to exclude labour and energy costs; these are difficult to allocate precisely to a particular contract. In addition the purchaser needs to be protected from liability for the supplier's costs in respect of any new equipment and machinery it chose to purchase to carry out the contract. The reasoning here is that the supplier will have the benefit of such items in carrying on its general business.

It is customary to provide that the cancellation claim shall never exceed the contract price of the goods concerned although this should not be necessary as the liability of a purchaser who refuses to accept delivery should never be more then the price it would have paid had it honoured the contract and accepted delivery.

In addition to a termination for convenience clause (or perhaps instead of) the purchaser may find protection with a *limitation of liability* clause. This is a stated financial limit on the purchaser's liability for cancellation. The extent of this limit is a matter for negotiation but if such a clause (or indeed a termination for convenience clause) forms part of the purchaser's standard terms of business they are subject to scrutiny for reasonableness under the Unfair Contract Terms Act 1977 (see Chapter 11). Thus, where the contract price is large, yet the purchaser has a limit on its liability for cancellation of a very small amount, this might well be regarded as an unreasonable limitation of the purchaser's liability.

Much is said and written about *partnership* within the supply chain and at times it is tempting to dismiss it as yet another piece of jargon. But with sophisticated procurement, whether in the field of defence, civil engineering or elsewhere, it is unrealistic to imagine that a prime contractor is able to finalise its contract with its customer and then, and only then, involve its suppliers by making the necessary contracts with them.

In these circumstances the spirit of partnership has an important role to play. Consideration should be given to the following:

- involving suppliers in negotiations with the end customer – this allows them to form a view of how probable it is that real business may be gained;

- keeping them informed as to progress or lack of it;

- making contracts with a supplier which are subject to:
  - the end customer committing itself to buying; and
  - the supplier achieving a technical specification, charging a stated price and committing to a firm delivery date.

There is much to be said in favour of encouraging suppliers to suggest imaginative solutions to the problems.

CHAPTER 3

Formation of written contracts and the battle of the forms

When we talk of a *contract* most people instinctively think of a one-off document drafted for a particular transaction and signed at the end by both parties.

A variation on this is a free-standing document which is often referred to as a *framework agreement*. A document of this kind usually comes into existence where the parties have anticipated that they might wish to do business with one another in the future. Accordingly, they agree a set of contract terms which the purchaser can, if it wishes to procure something from the supplier, simply cross reference on another document (usually its standard purchase order) so:

> *100 widgets at £10.00 each plus VAT.*
>
> *Delivery to be within three months of date of purchase order.*
>
> *Terms of contract are those contained in our framework agreement dated 1 June 2000 and these terms shall apply to the exclusion of the printed terms on the reverse of this purchase order.*

It must be remembered, however, that the purchase order described above will be no more than the purchaser's offer to buy; if the supplier no longer favours the terms in the framework agreement it can refuse to accept the offer. Similarly if the purchaser does not wish to buy in accordance with the framework agreement it can offer to buy on different terms.

Another way of making a written contract is by an exchange of correspondence. To understand such a contract it will be necessary to look at all the relevant letters, faxes or e-mails.

We now come to the most common way of purchasing: on the supplier's written *standard terms of sale* or the purchaser's *standard terms of purchase*. It is almost certain that the former will have been drafted to protect the supplier and the latter drafted to protect the purchaser.

More often than not a routine commercial purchase contract will be formed as follows:

1. The parties will have reached agreement on the major elements of the contract including price, delivery and the nature of the goods and/or services to be provided:

> *100 widgets at £10.00 each plus VAT.*
>
> *Delivery to be within three months of date of purchase order.*

2. The purchaser will then issue its standard purchase order. The front of this document will contain the particulars referred to in 1 and will also tell the supplier how it should accept the purchase order, perhaps by filling in a tear-off slip or sending a letter. In addition, there will be words on the front of the purchase order informing the supplier that the transaction will be governed by the standard terms of business on the back. On the back there will be a generic set of terms usually drafted to cover any kind of procurement, for all goods or for all services, or for both. It will nearly always be apparent that the draftsman's prime consideration is to protect the purchaser.

3. The supplier, after receipt of the document described in 2, does as it is asked and indicates its acceptance of the purchase order.

If all these things happen there is clearly a binding contract. The purchase order described at 2 is an offer which the supplier has accepted, *without reservation*, as described in 3.

Alas, life is not so simple! Communications can break down and then the *battle of the forms* begins:

Example 1   The supplier ('S') after receiving the purchase order writes back to the purchaser ('P'): 'We are pleased to supply the widgets at the price and within the delivery schedule specified by you. We have pleasure in enclosing our standard terms which shall govern this sale.'

P does not reply, or

Example 2   S never makes an acknowledgement of the purchase order.

Let us assume that in both examples S duly delivers the widgets to P but it later turns out the goods are defective. It is likely that if the contract was subject to S's terms, P may be in a worse position than if P's terms governed as S's terms will have been drafted so as to protect S.

Example 1 consists of an *offer* by P to buy on P's standard terms. S responds with a *counter offer* to sell on S's standard terms. P is not obliged to answer this counter offer, but P's acceptance of delivery is deemed to be an *acceptance* of S's offer to sell on S's standard terms.

Example 2 consists of an *offer* by P to buy on its standard terms. S is not under a duty either to accept or reject this offer. S is perfectly entitled to stay silent but *delivery* by S of the widgets amounts to an *acceptance* of P's *offer* to buy on P's terms.

In Example 2 it also follows that if a significant period of time passes before S delivers, P might well be entitled to refuse delivery upon the basis that acceptance of an offer (in this case the attempted delivery) must be made within a reasonable time and three months might well be regarded as too long.

It can be seen in both examples that *the winner of the battle of the forms is the last person to produce its standard terms.* In Example 2 P was the *only* one to produce its terms. A further example can be seen in the case of *Butler* v *Ex-Cell-O Corp.* (see Appendix).

Sometimes suppliers will try to impose their terms by printing them on their invoice or some other document such as a delivery note which comes with the goods at the time of delivery.

We can feel safe that contract terms contained on an invoice may be ignored. This is a document produced *after* the contract has been formed and the supplier cannot, at this stage, introduce new rules.

The delivery note is more of a worry. If, in Example 2, at the time of delivery the supplier says: 'Here are the goods you wanted. You can take them or leave them, but if you take them you do so on my terms, a copy of which you will find printed on the delivery note', then, if the purchaser does take the goods, the contract will be subject to the supplier's terms.

On the other hand, if this statement has not been made and the purchaser only finds the delivery note after he has accepted delivery, then the supplier would be deemed to have introduced its terms after the act of delivery which was the supplier's acceptance of an offer to buy on the purchaser's terms.

A good example of an attempt to introduce a term, an exemption clause, after the contract was made is to be found in the case of *Olley* v *Marlborough Court Hotel*:

> Mr and Mrs Olley checked in at the hotel reception desk and then went to their room. There was a notice in the room which excluded the hotel's liability for loss or damage to

guests' property. Due to the negligence of the hotel staff a thief was able to enter the Olleys' bedroom and steal a number of articles including Mrs Olley's fur coat. It was held that the contract was complete before Mr and Mrs Olley went up to their room and it was too late for the hotel to slip in a term attempting to exclude its liability.

A further example may be found in the case of *Dillon* v *Baltic Shipping Company* (see Appendix).

Unfortunately the position may not always be as clear-cut. There are cases in which it has been held that where the parties have had previous dealings with one another and in those dealings the purchaser was aware of and did not object to the supplier's standard terms of business, then those terms govern future contracts.

Cases always turn on their particular facts and circumstances and the golden rule is: *never accept delivery until it is clear whose terms apply.*

CHAPTER 4

Negotiating the contract

Whether the negotiation is of an entire contract, word by word, or just discussion of changes in a few areas of an otherwise acceptable document, the golden rule is *prior preparation*. It is said that British commercial negotiators often seem ill prepared and that when there is a team of them they frequently argue in front of the supplier thereby exposing internal rifts which the other side cannot be blamed for exploiting.

The following advice is intended for an individual or a team carrying out a negotiation:

1. Before beginning negotiations with a prospective supplier find out what, if any, prior talks have taken place. Has, for example, anything been said or written by a colleague which could cause an unpleasant surprise when talks start? If it has, it is vital to know as soon as possible. If some ill-advised person has *given it*

---

away before the negotiations start it may be necessary to carry out some damage limitation. Quite often this means contacting the supplier and warning it that: '… we understand our Mr Bloggs said delivery times weren't crucial. Unfortunately he wasn't aware of the true situation. When we meet next week we will be seeking a very precise delivery schedule. I thought I'd let you know, straightaway, so you have a chance to think about it.'

This approach may be embarrassing but it is far better than to spring it on the supplier when both sides meet. If it *is* sprung upon the supplier it may well lead to accusations of being difficult for the sake of it and a resultant bad atmosphere.

2. A team should always have a leader. This does not mean that he or she is the only person who is allowed to speak at the meeting. Rather, a leader should act as the focal point of the team. It is, for example, the team leader who should take the initiative in asking for breaks so that members can discuss matters between themselves. It is also the leader's task to ensure that verbal agreement on each point is being accurately recorded in writing as the negotiation proceeds. It is *not* the team leader's function to disregard a concern of a team member nor to try to overrule that member in front of the supplier.

3. Then we come to personalities. Regrettably, it sometimes happens that within a negotiating team there are individuals who have a strong dislike of someone who is part of the other side's team. Ideally, such a person should not be present at the negotiation unless there is confidence that he or she will keep calm. Even if there is that confidence, there is still the risk that

the supplier's representative, who is the object of the dislike, may start trouble.

What if there is no choice and that individual must be there? Again, this is where prior preparation and good team leadership are vital. Before meeting the supplier it is important for team members to acknowledge to one another that there is a potential problem here and to devise strategies to ward off troubles. It may, for example, be sensible to say to the individual '... when we come to clause 8, let me deal with it – I've had your input and fully understand your position; if you and your opposite number get at each other's throats we'll find it counterproductive.' Needless to say this has to be done with great tact and the temptation should be avoided of giving the impression that the person concerned is an unpleasant, hysterical fool who can't be trusted in civilised society. Even if he (or she) is!

The reverse of this problem is where a member of the team thinks this particular supplier or its goods or services are so wonderful that there should be no attempt to disagree with any proposal it might make. This sometimes arises with colleagues in a technical field who get carried away with what the supplier has to offer. So keen are they to get their hands on the goods or services that they show impatience with any attempts to ensure that there be a good contract containing proper protection. It must be made clear to them that legal and commercial factors *are* important and are not to be treated dismissively.

4. What has been said so far, does assume there is a team. Many purchasers will not have the resources to field more than one negotiator. While it is easy to say nobody should ever carry out

negotiations of any significance on his own it has to be acknowledged that often there is no choice.

Where this is the position no one negotiating on their own should ever be ashamed to tell the other side that the discussion is taking a turn which is beyond their technical or legal competence or, indeed, beyond their authority. It is a good idea, before even setting out for the negotiation, to warn people that it may be necessary to contact them (possibly at home) to check their availability if this happens and to ensure they will have the necessary paperwork and data with them to answer questions they may be asked.

5. Whose draft should form the basis of the negotiation? Undoubtedly there are great advantages in starting to negotiate from one's own standard terms of purchase or from a draft one has prepared for the particular transaction. If the supplier is prepared to run along with this it is put on the defensive by having to seek out deviations from that document. It is always easier to give things away if they are dispensable than it is to fight for concessions from a supplier-biased draft contract. If the supplier pushes for its draft to form the basis of the negotiation this is an ideal time to remind it who is the customer. Suppliers don't like to be told they are being arrogant and heavy-handed.

For the purchaser to succeed in achieving the goal of its draft being the basis of negotiation it helps if the supplier is provided with a copy of it as early as possible before the meeting. By taking the initiative early, it makes it harder for the supplier later to say that it wants to work from its own document.

It is rarely, if ever, a good idea to produce a draft contract like a rabbit out of a hat and expect to start negotiations on it straightaway. To do this is likely to cause misunderstanding, ill temper and delays.

6. Assuming the purchaser's draft contract is used as the basis for negotiations how tough should it be?

   (a) It should reflect discussions and agreements in principle reached so far, subject to anything that may need to be claimed back (see the first point on Mr Bloggs above).

   (b) It should normally express the position the purchaser would *like* to reach rather than the final position it expects to agree – if the expectation is that the supplier will only agree to a 12-month warranty, the draft should express a longer period.

   (c) It should *not*, however, be an exercise in trying to make life uncomfortable and unpleasant for the supplier for the sake of it – more will be said in Chapter 6 on the absurdity of *overspecifying* the goods or services.

   (d) It should *not* be a word-for-word copy of a previous contract with the same supplier which had itself been the subject of negotiation resulting in the purchaser making concessions. If time has proved that those concessions have not hurt, they can always be made again but if they are included at the beginning then the supplier will only try to obtain more advantages this time around.

7. Be satisfied that any material statement which has been made by the supplier is, or will be, recorded in the contract. If it is not, then such a statement will not necessarily be regarded as a term of the contract. If this is the position, and the statement turns out to be false, it may only be possible to make a claim for misrepresentation and the law relating to misrepresentation is notoriously difficult. It is necessary, for example, to prove that the statement was a statement of fact which induced the purchaser to enter the contract. Further, if the statement was made orally, there is the matter of proof.

8. If the parties seem to be making no progress on reaching agreement on a particular clause it is often better to leave it, move on to other matters and come back to it later. By then the objections may not be as great as they had been earlier.

9. Ensure that those negotiating have all the management support they need. Reference was made earlier to a supplier exploiting a perceived rift in the purchaser's organisation. Whether it is a team negotiating or just one person, it is essential that the supplier does not succeed in the tactic of reporting resistance to someone higher up in the purchaser's organisation. It is not pleasant to be told: '… well, if you refuse to agree to this we will just have to talk to Mr X, one of your directors, and we think he will agree with us.'

   Unfortunately this tactic sometimes works if the purchasing organisation has senior managers who, through vanity, weakness or just a desire for a quiet life, will overrule their negotiators. There is no easy answer to this. The problem may be eased by making sure that, as early as possible, everyone concerned understands *why* a firm stand needs to be taken on a particular contract term and promises to support it. If, despite this, a negotiator is regularly undermined by someone senior there is a very easy answer: he or she needs to look for another job!

10. Much has been spoken and written about *partnership* as the relationship between suppliers and purchasers, and although some reference is made to it in Chapter 2, it is largely outside the scope of this book to comment on its validity. What, however, partnership does *not* mean is the purchaser basing its demands on a supplier solely on the following:

> 'We don't want to hear any objections from you. We're partners – you must support us.'

If a purchaser wishes to pass on some of the risks it has accepted in its own contract to its own subcontractors, then earlier consultation with those subcontractors should have taken place. *Partnership* is not a mantra to be chanted when there are no other cogent arguments in support of a negotiating position.

CHAPTER 5

Simplicity and clarity in contract drafting

Some people are blessed with the gift of writing clearly and concisely. Others are not – they struggle with, and are afraid of, putting concepts into writing. The following exercise is highly recommended as a way of improving the presentation of contracts:

> Take a document (it can be a contract, a long letter or whatever) and see if there are any words which are repetitive or which otherwise serve no purpose. Delete them. Then see if there are any words which can be replaced by shorter or simpler ones. Delete these as well. Compare the revised version with the original and see how much better it is.

This exercise is also a very useful training tool for new staff.

Here are some suggestions for improving contractual documentation:

1. Try to follow the basic rules that short paragraphs look better than long ones and that short sentences look better than long ones.

2. Break concepts down by tabulation. Compare the following:

    Clause 5

    Delivery of the four units shall be in four instalments with delivery of the first on 8 January 2001, the second on 5 February 2001, the third on 5 March 2001 and the last on 2 April 2001. Delivery is to be made between the hours of 9:00 am and 5:00 pm to the purchaser's premises at 1 Yellow Brick Road London SE1 2EX and the seller shall unload each unit onto a pallet (supplied by purchaser).

    with

    Clause 5

    5.1   The seller shall deliver one unit on each of the following dates:

    8 January 2001;
    5 February 2001;
    5 March 2001; and
    2 April 2001.

> 5.2 *Deliveries shall be made to the purchaser's premises at 1 Yellow Brick Road London SE1 2EX between the hours of 9:00 am and 5:00 pm.*
>
> 5.3 *The seller shall unload each unit onto a pallet supplied by the purchaser.*

Both clauses are acceptable but the second one is much easier to read.

3. The use of different paragraph widths improves the appearance of a contract and makes it *reader friendly*.

4. Defined terms are useful drafting tools. If the subject of the contract of sale is an *XYZ 1107 Horizontal Grinding Machine* it is useful, after having introduced its name into the contract, to give it a shorter name:

> an *XYZ 1107 Horizontal Grinding Machine (called 'the Machine')*.

The effect of this is that, from then on, the contract needs just to refer to the *Machine* and it is clear what is meant.

The defined term described above is sometimes referred to as *a nickname*. In complex contracts there is often one clause (usually at the beginning) which defines the terms which are later to be used. Here is an example:

> 1. *In this contract, unless the context otherwise requires:*
>
> 1.1 *'Catering Services' shall mean those services set out in the attached schedule;*

1.2 'Contract Supervisor' shall mean the person nominated by the customer as responsible for the day-to-day supervision of the Catering Services; …

1.3 etc.

1.4 etc.

A clause like this serves as the contract's dictionary and, like any other dictionary, should be in alphabetical order.

5. Certain definitions are unnecessary because of section 61 of the Law of Property Act 1925:

In all deeds, contracts … unless the context otherwise requires –

(a) 'Month' means calendar month;

(b) 'Person' includes a corporation;

(c) The singular includes the plural and vice versa;

(d) The masculine includes the feminine and vice versa.

6. There is no need to state the obvious. All seasoned contract draftsmen have their favourite examples. Here is one from a draft contract prepared only a few years ago:

All references to dates in this agreement refer to the Gregorian calendar and not to the Julian calendar.

The last country to use the Julian calendar was Russia and it changed over to the Gregorian as long ago as 1918! This is perhaps an extreme example but here is one phrase which is frequently seen:

Unless the parties otherwise mutually agree, delivery shall be made on or before 2 April 2001.

The parties are always free to amend their agreement and there is no need to say *unless the parties otherwise mutually agree.* Taken to its logical limit every single provision in a contract would be prefaced by these words.

If for some reason this proviso is to be included then, at least, delete the word *mutually.* It is of the essence of any agreement that it is mutual.

7. Here is another bad habit:

    In the event that the supplier is unable to deliver due to circumstances beyond its control ...

Why not say:

    If the supplier is unable to deliver due to circumstances beyond its control ...?

8. Is it better to say:

    The seller shall ...

or

    The seller will ...?

The answer is *shall.* The duties of a contract party are imperatives and it is correct English to express third-party imperatives as *shall.*

Take care to distinguish between the expression of a duty as *shall* and the right to exercise a discretion which is expressed as *may*. A good example is to be found in section 15A of the Sale of Goods Act 1979:

> *... then, if the buyer does not deal as consumer, the breach is not to be treated as a breach of condition but may be treated as a breach of warranty.*

Here, *may* is correct: the buyer does not *have* to claim damages for a breach of warranty but *may* do so if it chooses. Where *may* is appropriate, then use it, rather than say *... has the right to.* This is clumsy.

9. Be consistent. If the contract is referred to as *this agreement*, then do not elsewhere call it *this contract*. It is confusing (particularly for foreign suppliers) and may result in an unwarranted suspicion there is some devious reason behind the change.

10. Try to avoid unnecessary work. Some draftsmen believe that every contract must have:
    – an index;
    – clause headings; and
    – a recital.
    Where the contract is long or the subject rather complex these can be useful, but with a fairly simple agreement it is worth considering whether these additions achieve anything.

11. If the contract is complex a recital may help. A recital is a piece of narrative which usually is inserted after the names of the parties and before the contract clauses. It is a convention that it

starts with the rather archaic '*WHEREAS*' and, after it, the contract clauses are introduced with the words '*IT IS AGREED:*'. It is also a convention that these are in bolder type. Here is an example:

(Details of the parties)

WHEREAS:
  A. *The parties possess expertise in their respective fields of mechanical engineering and plastics technology.*
  B. *They wish to collaborate with one another upon the development and production of an injection moulding machine.*
  C. *They wish to conduct the collaboration through the medium of a jointly owned company.*

IT IS AGREED:
Clause 1... ...

Nowadays the main reason for having a recital is that it provides a very brief summary of the purpose of the contract.

The words in the recital do not form part of the contract terms and a court will usually only be prepared to look at these words to see if they might resolve an ambiguity or obscurity in the terms of the contract.

12. Avoid archaic expressions such as:

In witness whereof the parties have hereunto set their hands ...

This gem can be safely replaced with:

Signed on behalf of ...

Here is another one worth avoiding:

... a full description of the goods is set forth in the schedule ...

Set out is better than *set forth*.

13. When it comes to signatures it is sufficient for *one* representative of each party to sign. There is no need for their signatures to be witnessed by anyone else.

14. Try to avoid the following:

    The parties are agreed that delivery shall be prior to 1 July 2001; The seller undertakes to make delivery prior to 1 July 2001; and The seller shall be responsible for making delivery prior to 1 July 2001.

    The contract is an agreement and the terms of it are the undertakings and responsibilities of the parties; all that need be said is:

    Delivery shall be prior to 1 July 2001.

15. Consider singulars and plurals. A company is singular and should be called *it* not *they*.

16. Here are some *anxiety expressions* commonly found in contracts – they serve no purpose and may safely be shortened:

    Each and every unit delivered shall be painted white.

    It is hard to see what *and every* adds to *each*. The same result is achieved with:

Each unit delivered shall be painted white.

No deliveries whatsoever shall be made at weekends.

Try

No deliveries shall be made at weekends.

The purchase price (fixed) of the goods is £1,000.

The addition of *(fixed)* is superfluous; the price is the price unless there is a prior course of dealing between the parties in which the supplier was allowed to increase its price or an express contract clause which allows a variation.

The supplier shall conform strictly with all its obligations under this contract.

This provision should not be necessary. A properly drafted contract should, in respect of each obligation, make it clear that the party subject to that obligation is mandated to comply with it. The possible exception is compliance with delivery dates for goods or compliance with the time for performance of services, where these words may help. But this is using a hammer to crack a nut. It is better, with delivery, to have words which expressly provide that failure to keep to agreed times allows the purchaser the right to treat the contract as repudiated as well as to claim damages. This will be discussed more fully in Chapter 15.

17. The use of numerals or words to express numbers. Should it be 8 or *eight?*

It is a well-established rule that numbers one to nine inclusive are expressed in words and numbers from 10 onwards are expressed in figures. However, this rule may be broken for the sake of consistency as it is in this book, where the first chapter is called *Chapter 1* and the last is *Chapter 20*. To change horses in mid-stream at Chapter 10 would be pedantic, messy and confusing.

Some people make a point of using both: *4,000 (four thousand) units.* If the parties to the contract feel there is a danger of the true number (4,000) being wrongly expressed as *40,000* or some other number and that to repeat the numerals with the words may avoid that mistake then there is nothing wrong in doing so. If the figures and the words are inconsistent then a court will usually decide that the words prevail over the figures.

18. Contracts should be expressed in the *active* and not the *passive* voice. Here are examples of the difference:

    – *the seller shall deliver the goods not later than 14 December 2001*
    – *the goods shall be delivered by the seller not later than 14 December 2001*

The first is in the active voice and the second is in the passive. The active voice is more positive and more appropriate for the expression of firm, contractual obligations and uses fewer words.

19. Keep any *choice of law clause* simple. It is not necessary to say:

> *This contract shall be interpreted and construed in accordance with English law.*

It is quite sufficient to say:

> *This contract shall be subject to English law.*

20. Take particular care with *notices clauses*. Contracts often require or allow a party to serve a notice on the other. Unless the notice is personally delivered to the other (and, ideally, a receipt obtained for it) there is a risk that the other party may later deny receiving it. If it is sent by post, then recorded delivery should be used. The clause should always set out the method of serving notices.

A problem comes with electronic transmission. If the notice is crucial, consideration should be given to providing, in the clause itself, that a notice sent by fax or electronic mail is deemed to have been received upon the expiry of a stated number of hours from transmission. Further discussion of this will be found in Chapter 18.

The suggestions above are not intended to be exhaustive. If the exercise described at the beginning of this chapter is carried out, others will emerge.

Remember always that if the style of contract drafting is clear and concise it will gain respect for the purchase function.

CHAPTER 6

The specification

A contract may be for the supply of goods or services or for both. It will be seen in the next two chapters that with goods, the supplier is under an implied duty to ensure they correspond with their description and that with services the supplier must use reasonable care and skill in performing those services.

What goods? What services? It is the contract specification which sets out details of what is to be supplied. Only by reference to this part of the contract can it be understood whether or not there has been compliance with the implied duties referred to above.

A widespread but very bad habit of those responsible for the preparation of a purchase contract is to regard the specification as a document to be drafted and agreed solely by their technical colleagues. They see their own function as merely to take that document and either to incorporate it into the text of the draft contract or, as is often done, to attach the specification to the back of the draft as an appendix.

This approach is simply not satisfactory. Although it is true that a specification may contain detail of a technical nature which those in the purchasing area cannot reasonably be expected to understand in depth, they nevertheless have the following duties prior to contract finalisation:

1. To make it crystal clear to the experts who are responsible for the contract specification that all the purchaser gets for its money is what is set out in the specification. This is a good opportunity to ask these technical colleagues whether there is any quality or feature they expect the supplier to include in the goods and/or services which is not dealt with in the specification.

   This question may flush out whether there have been any promises made by the supplier which have not found their way into the document. If there have been, those promises should be included.

2. To ensure that the specification is sufficiently definite. It is important to be suspicious of expressions such as these:

   – *The equipment has been designed to operate at 16,000 rpm.*
   – *The equipment has been tested at speeds of 16,000 rpm.*
   – *The equipment is capable of a speed of 16,000 rpm.*

   The experts need to be asked: 'At what speed do you need the equipment to operate?' If the answer is *16,000 rpm* then the specification needs to say:

   The equipment shall operate at 16,000 rpm.

3. To scrutinise closely the specification for gaps. It is a cause for concern if the experts expect the specification to become part of the contract before it is complete. For example, it is a frequent, but dangerous practice to use the abbreviation 'TBA' (to be agreed). A contract is the agreement. It is not part of an agreement with the rest to come into existence in the future. To leave a critical matter undetermined may result in the contract being invalid – *May and Butcher* v *R* (see Appendix).

4. To make sure the specification recognises any peculiarities of the goods and/or services that are being purchased. For example, suppose what is being bought is to be sold on to a customer in the Middle East. Will the goods work satisfactorily in the much higher ambient temperatures there? Is there a need for any written instructions on the goods to be written in Arabic? The specification should recognise, expressly, the particular purpose for which the goods or services are intended.

5. To see if there are matters contained in the specification which are also covered in other parts of the contract. It is not uncommon to find matters relating to delivery schedules or to defects in materials or workmanship in the specification itself. They should not be there because such matters do not relate to the description of the goods or services which is the purpose of the specification. If such matters appear in both documents (where the specification is an attachment to the contract) and there is conflict between the two, then there may be a real problem.

6. To consider the special position of specifications for goods which contain references to performance as in 2 above: *The equipment shall operate at 16,000 rpm.* If this statement is in the specification it is part of the description of the goods and, as will be seen in the next two chapters, if the goods do not correspond with this description then, as appropriate, the Sale of Goods Act 1979 and the Supply of Goods and Services Act 1982 may allow the purchaser a right to reject them as nonconforming. It will also be seen, however, that this right to reject does not last long.

The duration of a right to reject in respect of performance shortfall is complex but everything points to the need for there to be some stage when both supplier and purchaser can say safely: 'The goods are specification compliant and any claim the purchaser may now have must be based upon defects in workmanship or materials.'

One way of dealing with this is for the contract to include an acceptance test which sets out what must be tested, the time in which those tests must be performed and what level of performance must be demonstrated. It should then be stated that if the test results are met then the purchaser is deemed to have accepted the goods – that is, it has lost its right to reject the goods.

7. To be sure that in a contract for services sufficient details of the services are set out in the specification and that it is clear to the supplier whether there is anything out of the ordinary. When contracting for the procurement of catering services will the caterer be able to cope with any special dietary requirements of

foreign visitors? For further discussion on contracts for services see Chapter 9.

8. To make sure that the experts have not *overspecified* the goods or services. This was touched on in Chapter 4. There can sometimes be a fine line between *tough* contracting and *over-aggressive* contracting. When a purchaser seeks to write a specification so that it requires:

   – *the unachievable*; or
   – *the unnecessary*

this is over-aggressive. The specification is there to commit the supplier to meeting the purchaser's needs – it should not be used to demonstrate the purchaser's power.

It should not be worded in such a way that the supplier will either have to incur pointless expenditure or will almost certainly end up in breach of contract. Unfortunately, there seems to be a growing culture of just this. Purchasing organisations (particularly, it seems, government departments) are requiring, for example, levels of packaging far greater than they need and performance guarantees far in excess of real requirements. It is not just unprofessional, it may increase the price, extend delivery time and introduce complexity which is not needed.

If there is a specification requirement which may appear to a supplier to be unnecessary or unreasonable the requirement should be accompanied by an explanation as to *why* it is a requirement.

CHAPTER 7

The Sale of Goods Act 1979

There will be very few people involved with purchase contracts who will not have heard of this statute and it is likely many will have a copy in the office. If they do, it is also likely to be out of date. The Sale of Goods Act 1979 ('the SGA') has been amended by three later pieces of legislation: the *Sale and Supply of Goods Act 1994*, the *Sale of Goods (Amendment) Act 1994* and the *Sale of Goods (Amendment) Act 1995*. No further reference needs to be made to these as their effect is to incorporate amendments into the SGA.

Does this mean it is necessary to have a copy of the SGA *and* the three amendment statutes? No, there is a much easier way. A good legal bookshop (or the student bookshop at a nearby university) should have in stock books containing all the legislation in force in a particular field, updated to include the various amendments. It is important, however, to keep alert to future changes in legislation.

The SGA was first enacted in 1893. Even then it did not contain anything earth-shatteringly new. It was a clear (generally) and concise attempt to put into statutory form most of the rules relating to contracts for the sale of goods which, until then, had to be looked for in the recorded decisions of the judges.

To what contracts does the SGA apply?

The SGA applies to *a contract of sale of goods* which is defined as:

> ... a contract by which the seller transfers or agrees to transfer the property in goods to the buyer for a money consideration called the price.
>
> (section 2(1))

Thus it *does not* apply to contracts:

- for the hire of goods;

- for services;

- for the supply of both goods *and* services;

- where no money changes hands (for example a straight *swap* or *barter*);

- for the sale of land.

The first four exceptions will be considered in Chapter 8. The last exception (sale of land) is outside the scope of this book.

What does the SGA do?

Where there is a contract for the sale of goods the SGA provides a fairly comprehensive set of rules governing the respective rights and duties of the parties.

Section 55(1) makes it clear that the rights and duties implied by it, and implied by the law generally, may be varied by the express agreement of the parties, by the course of dealing between the parties or by custom and practice. Further consideration of section 55 will be found towards the end of this chapter.

It is not the purpose of this chapter to provide a comprehensive analysis, section by section, of the SGA's provisions, but to highlight the more important parts for those dealing with purchase contracts. For the rest of it the parties are called *seller* and *buyer* as these are the terms used in the SGA. All references to section numbers are to sections of the SGA unless stated otherwise.

Formalities

A contract for the sale of goods may be made in writing, orally or by conduct (section 4(1)).

Price

The price of the goods need not be expressed in the contract – it may be fixed in a manner set out in the contract or determined by the course of dealing between the parties (section 8(1)).

Accordingly, the contract may provide that the price shall be fixed by an independent valuer or the price may be a price fixed by a particular commodity market on a certain day.

Where the price is not determined under section 8(1) then section 8(2) provides:

> … the buyer must pay a reasonable price.

Generally, the law of contract requires the parties to be reasonably clear about their principal duties before they are treated as contractually bound, but this is an exception. If no price is fixed and later they fail to agree on a price a court will decide it for them. Reference should be made to the case of *May and Butcher* v *R* in the Appendix.

Conditions and warranties

Section 11 deals with the different remedies available where there is a breach of a term which is a *condition* and the breach of a term which is a *warranty*.

If there is a breach of the former then the innocent party may choose to reject the goods and treat the contract as repudiated (that is, discharged) and, in addition, sue for any damages it has suffered. Alternatively it may elect to let the contract continue and sue for damages.

If, however, the term is a warranty then there is no right to reject the goods and the innocent party only has a claim for damages (if any) it has suffered.

Whether a term is a condition or a warranty is a matter of construction of the contract (section 11(3)) but it will be seen that in the case of some of the terms implied by the SGA, the statute specifies which are conditions and which are warranties.

The effect of the buyer *accepting* the goods is that it loses the right to reject them for a breach of condition and is left with only a right to claim for any damages suffered (section 11(4)). More will be said later (in the section on quality and fitness in this chapter) about *acceptance* of goods. The case of *Wallis, Son & Wells* v *Pratt and Haynes* (see Appendix) provides useful commentary on section 11(4).

The distinction between conditions and warranties must always be viewed against a background that sometimes a buyer may see the right to reject the goods as all important and the ability to claim damages as unimportant. In other cases the position is quite the reverse. Here is an example of each:

• When goods are delivered to the buyer it is discovered that there is something about them which would entitle the buyer to reject them – for example, because they do not conform with their description. This right to reject may be important to the buyer, not because the nonconformance is insurmountable but because, since the contract was made, the buyer has discovered that it can buy similar goods elsewhere, at a lower price. It will be seen later that the right of a buyer to reject for an ulterior motive has been somewhat limited by an amendment to the SGA in the form of a new section 15A which deals with slight breaches.

- The buyer buys a spare part for £1 and fits it into a machine worth £250,000. The spare part is defective and destroys the machine. Here, a right to reject the spare part is unimportant – what the buyer wants is damages to compensate it for the destruction of the machine.

Title

The fundamental characteristic of a sale of goods is that *title* in the goods passes from seller to buyer. Title, more generally known as *ownership*, is the greatest right anyone can have in a personal chattel. Without title, and subject to a few exceptions, if the seller does not transfer title to the buyer the buyer cannot sell the goods on to anyone else.

Accordingly, section 12(1) provides that there is an implied *condition* that the seller will have a right to sell the goods or it will obtain that right by the time when title is due to pass from seller to buyer.

Section 12(2) implies *warranties*:

(a) that at the time title passes to the buyer, the goods will be free from any charge or encumbrance not disclosed or known to the buyer at the time of the contract; and

(b) the buyer will *enjoy quiet possession* of the goods except for any disturbance of this right by any person entitled to a charge or encumbrance known to the buyer at the time of the contract.

The above is a paraphrase of section 12(2) and this subsection is unlikely to feature in the activities of many purchasers. Two examples provide sufficient explanation:

- if the goods are subject to some kind of charge or lien in favour of a creditor of the seller, there is a breach;

- if the goods infringe a third party's trade mark so that the buyer may only resell the goods after removing the trade mark, there is also a breach.

Other subsections deal with the seller's duties in the rare position where either the seller sells goods but is only able to transfer limited title, the goods being subject to a charge or encumbrance, or where the buyer's right to enjoy quiet possession may be limited. In these circumstances the seller is obliged to make disclosure of any such defect in title before the contract is made.

Correspondence with description

Section 13(1) is short and to the point:

> Where there is a contract for the sale of goods by description, there is an implied term that the goods will correspond with the description.

Section 13(1A) provides that under English law the term implied is a *condition*, thereby giving the buyer a right to reject the goods and treat the contract as repudiated.

Under section 13(2), even if the buyer had seen an accurate sample, there is still a breach of the implied condition if the goods supplied do not correspond with the contract description.

In one case the buyer, a farmer, had bought seed described as *sunflower* seed which turned out to be *marigold* seed. There was a breach of section 13(1) even though the seed supplied conformed with the sample seen by the farmer at the time the contract was made. The sample, of course, was of marigold seed.

Section 13(3) provides that *there may still be a sale by description even if the buyer has seen the goods before sale and selected them.*

This part of the chapter should be read in conjunction with Chapter 6 (on the specification) as the specification is that part of a written contract which contains the description of the goods.

Quality and fitness

The SGA retains the basic principle of the sanctity of the business bargain – if a party makes a bad one, then so be it. This philosophy is seen in section 14(1):

> Except as provided by this section and section 15 below and subject to any other enactment, there is no implied term about the quality or fitness for any particular purpose of goods supplied under a contract of sale.

It is often expressed in the maxim *caveat emptor* – let the buyer beware. Important exceptions to caveat emptor are to be found in sections 14 and 15.

Section 14 implies two *conditions* as to quality and fitness into contracts for the sale of goods provided the seller sells '... *in the course of a business* ...' If the seller is a private individual disposing of his own motor car then clearly he is not subject to the two conditions. But a seller will be subject to them even if his disposal of the goods is *incidental* to his main business such as a fisherman who sells his boat because he wants to buy a new one.

Under section 14(2) there is an implied condition that the goods '... *are of satisfactory quality*'.

Section 14(2A) makes it clear that what is *satisfactory* is to be judged objectively and that the goods meet this requirement:

> ... if they meet the standard that a reasonable person would regard as satisfactory ...

Account has to be taken of such matters as the age of the goods – what may amount to satisfactory quality in second-hand goods may not be satisfactory quality in new goods.

Section 14(2B) provides a non-exhaustive list of aspects relating to quality:

(a) fitness for all the purposes for which goods of the kind in question are commonly supplied,
(b) appearance and finish,
(c) freedom from minor defects,
(d) safety, and
(e) durability.

Further limitations are imposed by section 14(2C) which provides that the condition will not be implied where the aspect which causes the goods to be unsatisfactory is either:

- one specifically drawn to the buyer's attention before the contract is made; or

- where the buyer examines the goods before the contract is made and the examination should have revealed the defect; or

- where the sale is by sample and a reasonable examination of the sample would have revealed the defect.

The second condition, which is implied by section 14(3), is that where the buyer sells in the course of a business and, *expressly or by implication*, makes known to the seller any *particular* purpose for which the goods are being bought, the goods must be *reasonably fit for that purpose*. However, this condition is not implied where the circumstances show that either the buyer has not relied on the seller's skill and judgement or that it would be unreasonable for the buyer to so rely. The following examples may help:

- The buyer ('B') buys a plastic water tank which the seller ('S') has said, in answer to a question from B, is suitable for the storage of hot water. B soon finds that exposure of the tank to hot water is causing it to melt. Here there has been a reliance on S's skill and judgement and the particular purpose for which the goods are required has been expressly made known to S. The condition is implied.

- Had B not made it clear the tank was intended for use with *hot* water, it would be a question of fact whether or not such use was by implication known to S and hence whether the condition is implied into the contract.

- Here the facts are the same, except that when B asks S if it is suitable for use with hot water the reply is: 'I haven't a clue – you'd need to talk to the manufacturer.' If B goes ahead and buys it anyway, the condition is not implied into the contract because B has not relied on S's skill and judgement.

- Here the facts are the same except that this time B uses the tank to store sulphuric acid with disastrous consequences. S has not been informed of this proposed use. The condition is not implied.

Sales by sample

Section 15 provides another exception to caveat emptor:

(1) A contract of sale is a contract for sale by sample where there is an express or implied term to that effect in the contract.

(2) In the case of a contract for sale by sample there is an implied term –
   (a) That the bulk will correspond with the sample in quality;
   (b) ...
   (c) That the goods will be free from any defect, making their quality unsatisfactory, which would not be apparent on reasonable examination of the sample.

(3) ... the term implied by subsection (2) above is a condition.

Subsection (1) makes clear that not every contract where the buyer has seen an *example* of the goods is necessarily a sale by sample. The contract either has to say it is or there must be an implication arising from the surrounding circumstances.

If a contract is not a sale by sample, this will not matter to a disappointed buyer who can rely upon the term implied by section 14(2), provided the seller is selling in the course of a business. Section 15 applies to contracts whether or not the seller is selling in the course of a business.

It is perhaps curious that section 15 refers to a *term* in the singular whereas, on the face of it, 2(a) and 2(c) impose separate and distinct conditions. The reported cases, however, have taken the view that the seller need not be in breach of both (a) *and* (c) – a breach of (a) *or* (c) is sufficient.

In a case called *Godley* v *Perry* a boy of six was blinded in one eye by a plastic catapult. When he went to use it the toy snapped and either a piece of plastic from it or the stone he intended to fire struck him. In litigation between the retailers, the wholesaler and the importer there was never any suggestion that to succeed under section 15(2) it was necessary to prove a breach of both (a) and (c). Liability there was based solely upon a breach of (c).

In that case the court took a relaxed approach to the requirement that the failure as to quality must not be apparent on a reasonable examination of the sample. The judge said that it was not necessary for a prospective buyer to try to test the sample to destruction. The test which was carried out by the shopkeeper (pulling back the elastic) was a reasonable examination even though it did not reveal the defects, which were that the goods were made of cheap, brittle plastic which was then badly moulded.

Slight breaches: restrictions on rejection

Although a breach of any of the terms implied by sections 13 to 15 gives the buyer the right to reject the goods, this right is now restricted by a new section 15A, added to the SGA in 1995 and intended to deal with the problem of the buyer described earlier in this chapter who wishes to reject for an ulterior motive.

An example is to be found in a case called *Arcos Ltd* v *Ronaasen*, decided in the 1930s under the 1893 Act. There, the contract specification for timber said it should be half an inch thick. Most of the timber delivered was, in fact, very slightly thicker (by about 1/16 of an inch) but was quite suitable for the buyer's purpose. The court felt bound to uphold the buyer's right to reject for breach of the implied condition that the goods should correspond with description, even though the buyer's real reason for rejection was that by the time of delivery it could get a similar product for a lower price elsewhere.

Section 15A, subsections (1), (2) and (3), are worded as follows:

(1) Where in the case of a contract of sale –
   (a) the buyer would, apart from this subsection, have the right to reject goods by reason of a breach on the part of the seller of a term implied by sections 13,14 or 15 above, but
   (b) the breach is so slight that it would be unreasonable for him to reject them,
   then, if the buyer does not deal as consumer, the breach is not to be treated as a breach of condition but may be treated as a breach of warranty.

(2) This section applies unless a contrary intention appears in, or is to be implied from, the contract.

(3) It is for the seller to show that a breach fell within subsection (1)(b) above.

Subsection (1) makes it clear that this limitation does not apply to a buyer who *deals as consumer.*

Subsection (2) allows the parties to exclude section 15A from the contract thus enabling a buyer to reject even where the breach is slight. This may be achieved by these words in the contract:

> *The provisions of section 15A(1) of the Sale of Goods Act 1979 shall not apply to this contract.*

It will be seen in Chapter 11 that the provisions of the Unfair Contract Terms Act 1977 can conceivably be used by a seller against a buyer. In the absence of subsection (2) a buyer who attempted to shelter behind the above words which negate section 15A(1) might be required to justify the reasonableness of the exclusion.

Subsection (3) places the onus of proof upon the seller to show that the breach is so slight that it is unreasonable for the buyer to reject the goods.

Even if the contract does exclude the provisions of section 15A(1) this may not help the buyer. There is a Latin maxim *de minimis non curat lex* (the law is not concerned with trifles). For example, in the timber case referred to above, the court talked of deviations from specification which might be so very small that they would not be regarded as a breach of the implied term. As to the conditions implied by section 14(2), section 14(3) and section 15(2) it would follow that if the defects were so insignificant that they would not render unsatisfactory the quality of the goods or make the goods unfit for purpose, there would not be a breach of them.

Transfer of title and risk

Section 12 of the SGA (see the section on title of this chapter above) deals with the seller's obligation to transfer good title. It is also important to know *when* title passes from seller to buyer because:

- when title has passed to a buyer who fails to pay the contract price, the seller may sue for that price (section 49(1));

- subject to some exceptions, a buyer cannot transfer good title to a third party unless he has good title;

- unless the parties agree otherwise, the risk of accidental loss or damage to the goods is borne by the party who has title (section 20). Thus if title has passed to the buyer and the goods are accidentally destroyed before delivery, the buyer still has to pay the price. Naturally, if the accident was caused by the seller's negligence, the buyer may sue for the tort of negligence.

Section 17 provides that in the case of identified goods, title (which it calls *the property*) is transferred to the buyer at *such time as the parties to the contract intend it to be transferred*. Accordingly, if the contract states the moment at which title shall pass, then that expresses the parties' intention. The parties might, for example, provide that title only passes when the seller has delivered the goods to the buyer or that title shall only pass when the buyer has paid for the goods.

In the absence of such an express intention, section 18 sets out certain rules for ascertaining the parties' intentions. The most important of these may be summarized as follows:

- Where the subject of the contract is *specific goods* (that is where the seller must supply the buyer with particular goods rather than any goods which answer a description) then title passes as soon as the contract is made.

- Where the subject of the contract is *unascertained goods* (where goods are not specific and the agreement to sell merely describes them) title passes when one party has *appropriated* goods for the performance of the contract, with the assent of the other. Usually appropriation will consist of the seller selecting an item from stock, which conforms with the contract description where the buyer is aware that the selection has been made. The buyer's assent will be implied by not objecting to the item selected.

Other rules deal with the passing of title in:

- goods which have to be weighed or measured to establish the price;

- goods on *sale or return*;

- goods which have to be separated from other items before delivery.

Although the basic rule is that unless the seller has good title he cannot transfer title, exceptions to this are to be found in sections 21, 23, 24 and 25. Further exceptions are to be found in other statutes.

Performance

Section 27 sets out three duties concerning performance of the contract:

- the duty of the seller to deliver;

- the duty of the buyer to accept delivery; and

- the duty of the buyer to pay.

The remainder of Part IV (sections 28 to 37) expands on the extent of these three duties if a problem arises which the contract has not provided for:

- Payment and delivery are concurrent. The buyer has no inherent right to credit (section 28).

- Delivery is at the seller's premises (section 29(2)).

- Delivery must be made within a reasonable time (section 29(3)).

- Delivery must take place at a reasonable hour (section 29(5)).

- If something needs to be done to put the goods into a deliverable state (for example, dismantling a piece of equipment so that an individual component of it may be delivered to the buyer) the expenses of doing this are to be borne by the seller (section 29(6)).

- Where the seller delivers a greater or lesser quantity than that contracted for, then the buyer may:

– in the case of a lesser quantity reject them or keep them – in the latter case the buyer must pay at the contract rate (section 30(1));

– in the case of a greater quantity, reject the whole or accept the contract amount and reject the rest. The buyer cannot insist on keeping the greater quantity (section 30(2)).

The right of the buyer in either case above to reject the whole amount is lost where the buyer is not a consumer and the shortfall or the excess *is so slight that it would be unreasonable for him to do so* (section 30(2A)). The reason for this subsection is similar to the reason for section 15A (see the section on slight breaches in this chapter above).

Again, the onus of proof is upon the seller to show that the shortfall or excess is so slight that rejection is unreasonable.

• Unless otherwise agreed, the seller, if asked by the buyer at the time of delivery, must allow the buyer a reasonable opportunity to examine the goods to ascertain whether they are in conformity with the contract and, where there is a sale by sample, to compare the bulk with the sample (section 34).

• It will be recalled that section 11(4) takes away a buyer's right to reject the goods for a breach of a condition when the goods have been *accepted*. Section 35(1) provides when acceptance by the buyer takes place:

(a) when he intimates to the seller that he has accepted them, or

(b) when the goods have been delivered to him and he does any act in relation to them which is inconsistent with the ownership of the seller.

The last part of (b) contains an oddity in its drafting. In the absence of a *Romalpa clause* (see Chapter 16) title to the goods will nearly always have passed from seller to buyer by delivery at the latest. If title has passed it is difficult to see how the buyer can do anything: '… inconsistent with the ownership of the seller …'

The better view is that these words really mean:

… inconsistent with the ability for ownership to revert to the seller …

Acceptance by the buyer may also occur under section 35(4):

… when after the lapse of a reasonable time he retains the goods without intimating to the seller that he has rejected them.

Section 35 is not easy to follow in so far as it takes away the right of rejection:

– when the buyer does anything to the goods inconsistent with the ownership of the seller; or

– when the buyer does not reject within a reasonable time.

One difficulty is that a buyer may only become aware that there is a breach of condition when something is done which is inconsistent with the ownership of the seller. A defect in raw materials which causes them not to be of satisfactory quality may only be capable of discovery when the materials are subject to an industrial process. The effect of that process on the goods, however, will make it impossible to return them to the seller in their original state.

A case called *Bernstein* v *Pamson Motors* is some authority for the proposition that a *reasonable time* may be short rather than long. There, the buyer was held to have lost his right to reject a new car which suffered a seized camshaft after only 135 miles and when only 29 days had elapsed between delivery and rejection. To make matters worse, the buyer was ill for some of this time when he did not even use the car!

In a more recent case, *Truk (UK) Ltd* v *Tokmakidis*, rejection of a truck lifting device was allowed over a year after delivery. It was held that in a case such as this, where goods are bought for resale, the buyer is able to reject within the time it reasonably took to resell them *plus* a further period to allow the sub-buyer to examine them and try them out.

The position is unclear and the advice given in Chapter 1 is repeated: *it is much better to have an express acceptance provision in a contract than to rely upon section 35.*

A prior request or agreement that the seller repairs the goods does not necessarily amount to acceptance, nor does delivery of the goods to a third party (section 35(6)).

- Section 35A gives to a buyer who has the right to reject defective goods a further right to accept some and to reject the rest.

Where the buyer lawfully rejects the goods then, unless otherwise agreed, it is for the seller to collect them; it is sufficient if the buyer notifies the seller of the refusal to accept them (section 36).

If the buyer does not take delivery he is liable to the seller for any loss occasioned and also for a reasonable charge for the care and custody of the goods (section 37).

Other matters

Various other subjects are dealt with in the SGA, including the rights of an unpaid seller and the right of a buyer to damages – some of these will be dealt with in other chapters.

Section 55 deserves special mention:

(1) Where a right, duty or liability would arise under a contract of sale of goods by implication of law, it may (subject to the Unfair Contract Terms Act 1977) be negatived or varied by express agreement, or by the course of dealing between the parties, or by such usage as binds both parties to the contract.

(2) An express term does not negative a term implied by this Act unless inconsistent with it.

Subsection (1) expresses the basic purpose of the SGA – it is there only to fill in gaps in a contract; if the parties wish to agree something different, then that is their right – subject only to other restrictions imposed by common law or statute. An example of the former is an exorbitant level of liquidated damages for late delivery which would be unenforceable as a penalty. An example of the latter is, of course, the Unfair Contract Terms Act 1977 (see Chapter 11).

CHAPTER 8

The Supply of Goods and Services Act 1982

In Chapter 7 it was seen that the Sale of Goods Act 1979 only applies to a contract for the sale of goods which is defined in section 2(1):

> A contract of sale of goods is a contract by which the seller transfers or agrees to transfer the property in goods to the buyer for a money consideration, called the price.

Accordingly, that Act does not apply to contracts for services, *mixed* contracts (where the supplier provides both goods and services), barter contracts or contracts for the hire of goods. Until the Supply of Goods and Services Act 1982 these were subject to common law. The 1982 Act (called, from now on, 'the SGSA') provides them with a statutory framework. It is not, however, anywhere near as comprehensive a framework as the 1979 Act.

Contracts for the transfer of goods

Sections 1 to 5A apply to a contract where title in goods is transferred from one party ('the transferor') to the other ('the transferee'), whether or not there is also the provision of services under the contract. Some contracts involving transfer of title are excluded by section 1(2):

(a) a contract of sale of goods;

(b) a hire-purchase agreement;

(c) a contract under which the property in goods is (or is to be) transferred in exchange for trading stamps on their redemption;

(d) a transfer or agreement to transfer which is made by deed and for which there is no consideration ...;

(e) a contract intended to operate by way of mortgage, pledge, charge or other security.

It will be noted that the SGSA, like the Sale of Goods Act 1979, uses the word *property* rather than *title* or *ownership*.

Section 2(1) provides that in contracts for the transfer of goods there is an implied condition that the transferor has or will have the right to transfer title in the goods to the transferee.

Other parts of section 2 deal with the rights of the transferee to take the goods free of charges and encumbrances and to enjoy *quiet possession* of the goods. Where the goods are affected by being subject, for example, to a lien, then disclosure of it must be made prior to contract.

Accordingly, section 2, as regards the obligation to transfer title etc., gives to a transferee rights similar to those given to a buyer by section 12 of the Sale of Goods Act.

What does not appear in the SGSA is any attempt to provide guidance as to when title is deemed to pass to the transferee. There is no equivalent of section 18 of the Sale of Goods Act 1979 in the SGSA. This leaves open, particularly with a contract for work and materials, when title to the goods becomes that of the transferee. When the contract is, for example, for the supply and installation of an air conditioning system, do the materials become the transferee's when the supplier first brings them on site? Or does title transfer only when they are installed? With contracts of this kind it is important that this matter be expressly agreed by the parties.

Section 3, again, is substantially similar to section 13 of the Sale of Goods Act. Where there is a contract for the transfer of goods by description there is an implied *condition* that the goods will correspond with the description. A transfer of goods by description is still subject to section 3:

- even if it is also a contract by sample and the bulk corresponds with the sample; and

- even if the goods have been exposed for supply and are selected by the transferee.

Section 4 of the SGSA, which implies conditions where the transferor is acting in the course of a business that the goods shall be of satisfactory quality and fit for purpose, closely tracks section 14 of the Sale of Goods Act.

Section 5 also closely follows section 15 of the Sale of Goods Act and implies a condition where there is a transfer of goods by reference to a sample:

(a) that the bulk will correspond with the sample in quality; and

(b) that the transferee will have a reasonable opportunity of comparing the bulk with the sample; and

(c) that the goods will be free from any defect making their quality unsatisfactory which would not be apparent on reasonable examination of the sample.

(section 5(2))

Subsection (b) above which appears in section 5 no longer appears in its counterpart section 15 of the Sale of Goods Act but is now to be found in section 34 of that Act.

There seems to be a similar problem with section 5 as there is with section 15 of the Sale of Goods Act, in that the implied condition appears to be made up of (a) plus (b) plus (c), but there could well be a breach of (c) without a breach of (a). It is, however, difficult to imagine how a breach of (b) could take place.

Section 5A(1) treats (a) and (c) as disjunctive and disregards (b) altogether:

(1) When in the case of a contract for the transfer of goods –

(a) the transferee would, apart from this subsection, have the right to treat the contract as repudiated by reason of a breach on the part of the transferor of a term implied by section 3, 4 or 5(2)(a) or (c) above, ...

Section 5A, once again, follows section 15A of the Sale of Goods Act in preventing a transferee from rejecting the goods for breach of a condition implied by section 3 (description), section 4 (quality and fitness) or section 5 (sample) where the breach is so slight that a termination would be unreasonable. The commentary in Chapter 7 on the purpose of section 15A of the Sale of Goods Act applies equally to section 5A of the SGSA. This section does not apply where the transferee deals as consumer.

Contracts for the hire of goods

Sections 6 to 10 deal with hire contracts. Section 6 excludes from the application of the Act hire purchase agreements or contracts where the consideration for the hire is the redemption of trading stamps. Both these kinds of transaction are subject to other statutory controls.

A contract for the hire of goods is:

> ... a contract under which one person bails or agrees to bail goods to another by way of hire ...
>
> (section 6(1))

The SGSA applies to contracts of hire whether or not services are also provided under the same contract and irrespective of the form of the consideration provided in exchange.

Section 7 follows section 12 of the Sale of Goods Act 1979 and section 2 of this Act by implying a condition that the bailor has the right to transfer *possession* to the bailee for the period of bailment.

There is further an implied warranty that during the hire period the bailee shall enjoy *quiet possession* of the goods.

Sections 8, 9, 10 and 10A introduce similar provisions for goods the subject of a contract of hire as for a contract for the sale of goods or a contract for the transfer of goods:

- implied conditions concerning correspondence with description and sample;

- implied conditions concerning quality and fitness for purpose; and

- the loss of a bailee's right to reject the goods for breach of one of these where the breach is so slight that rejection would be unreasonable

Contracts for the supply of services

A contract for the supply of a service is dealt with by sections 12 to 16 of the SGSA provided:

- it is a contract under which a supplier agrees to carry out a service;

- it is not a contract of service (employment) or apprenticeship.

A contract for services is still within the Act even though it also covers the transfer or bailment of goods (section 12(3)).

The Secretary of State is given the power to order by statutory instrument that one or more of sections 13 to 15 shall not apply to services of a description specified in the order and may make different provision in the order.

Section 13 deals with the quality of the service to be provided:

> In a contract for the supply of a service when the supplier is acting in the course of a business, there is an implied term that the supplier will carry out the service with reasonable care and skill.

Three points emerge from the above. Firstly the supplier must be acting in the course of a business. The Act gives no guidance as to what this means and neither does the Sale of Goods Act 1979 where this qualification also applies to the implied conditions of quality and fitness for purpose under section 14 of that Act.

The problem is that it is hard to imagine a contract for services where the supplier is not acting in the course of a business. Recipients will normally pay for what they get and the service provider, by reason of such payment, will normally be said to be acting in the course of a business. From the reported cases it is fairly clear that a supplier will be said to be acting in the course of a business even where that which is supplied is incidental to another business or is a *sideline*. Further mention of this is made in Chapter 9.

Secondly, what is implied is a *term*. As it is not classified as either a condition or a warranty the term is an *innominate term* – one where a breach of it may be slight or very serious. Only when the breach occurs may it be decided whether or not the innocent party may treat the contract as repudiated. This subject receives further treatment in Chapter 15.

Thirdly, the standard of care (*reasonable care and skill*) is much more restrained than in the sale or supply of goods, where the liability is strict. The service supplier's implied duty under section 13 is only to avoid negligence. With goods, the implied condition is that the seller or transferor *must* get it right. If there is something in the goods which renders them not of satisfactory quality the seller or transferor is in breach, even if he neither knew nor had the means of knowing there was anything wrong with the goods.

It follows from this that where something has gone wrong in a contract for both goods and services it must be established whether the fault was in the material the supplier used or in the supplier's workmanship. If it is the latter, negligence by the supplier will need to be established.

Section 14 deals with time for performance:

(1) Where, under a contract for the supply of a service by a supplier acting in the course of a business, the time for the service to be carried out is not fixed by the contract, left to be fixed in a manner agreed by the contract or determined by the course of dealing between the parties, there is an implied term that the supplier will carry out the service within a reasonable time.

(2) What is a reasonable time is a question of fact.

Although it is not possible to reject a service which has been badly performed it is possible to treat the contract as repudiated by the supplier who fails to provide the service. But treating the contract as repudiated needs to be handled with care. If the contract does not have a term stating when the service should commence the best and safest practice is to inform the supplier that the delay is now considerable and to state a reasonable time after which failure to commence will be regarded as the supplier's repudiation of the contract and also expose him to a claim for damages.

It is always best to have a definite starting date in the contract plus a provision that the contract may be terminated at any time by the customer if the service does not commence on that date.

Then there is the supplier who takes an extraordinarily long time to complete the service or the supplier who *loses interest* and never completes.

With the former, the starting place in establishing whether there is a liability is to look at the terms of the contract. Was the service to be started and completed within a stated period? If it was, then the supplier is in breach and would normally be liable unless there is a clause which gives a right to an extension if, for example, performance has been delayed through bad weather or to another circumstance beyond the supplier's control (see Chapter 15).

Where, as happens, the supplier shows no sign of ever finishing then the customer will be entitled to treat the contract as repudiated and claim damages. In the absence of an express contractual provision entitling the customer to terminate, it is wise to serve written notice of this which records the delay, the lack of activity and the intention to treat the contract as repudiated if work does not recommence within a stated (reasonable) period.

Section 15 provides that where the consideration for the supply of a service is not determined by the contract, left to be determined in a manner agreed by the contract (for example, a clause specifying that the consideration shall be fixed by an independent valuer) or determined by the course of dealing between the parties, there is an implied term that the customer shall pay a *reasonable price* – what this should be is a question of fact.

Excluding the Act

Section 11(1) (for transfer of goods and hire) and section 16(1) (in the case of services) allow the provisions of the SGSA to be negatived or varied by express agreement, dealing or usage, but this is subject to the Unfair Contract Terms Act 1977.

Further, an express term does not negative an implied term unless inconsistent with it.

Chapter 11 will examine the extent to which the 1977 Act limits the ability of the parties to exclude or restrict liability for breach of the express and implied terms of a contract.

CHAPTER 9

Contracts for services

Quality and scope

It will be recalled from Chapter 8 that section 13 of the Supply of Goods and Services Act 1982 provides:

> In a contract for the supply of a service where the supplier is acting in the course of a business, there is an implied term that the supplier will carry out the service with reasonable care and skill.

Unless there is a clear specification which sets out precise tasks the supplier discharges his contractual duty if he fulfils the statutory quality requirement by performing the services without negligence.

A common problem arises with contracts such as industrial cleaning contracts. If there is not a detailed specification there may be endless debate as to whether or not the cleaning has been carried out with reasonable care and skill. It is very much a matter of opinion. On the other hand, to specify every single action that must be performed will result in a very long document. Further, a very detailed specification, if followed to the letter, may result in dissatisfaction if the performers of the service *work to rule* and do not clean anything which is not provided for in the contract.

The following is an example:

> *All hallway and corridor floors shall be washed on Wednesday and Friday evenings.*

This may be fine. It may *not* be if, on Tuesday, it rains all day and by the evening the floor in the entrance hall is filthy. If the contract had been less specific the cleaners might well have cleaned it that evening *because it needed doing.* The answer may be to have a term such as:

> *All hallway and corridor floors shall be washed on Wednesday and Friday evenings and on any other evening when their condition requires it.*

This does provide some flexibility.

A purchaser drafting cleaning contracts and similar should seriously consider inclusion of the following:

- adequate supervision and inspection by the supplier;

- joint inspections by representatives of each side;

- the supplier to have duties to provide adequate equipment and materials;

- a designated area for storage of equipment and materials when not in use.

Many attempts have been made to regulate the quality of service contracts by using such devices as *service points*. The parties establish in their contract a regime in which the supplier's payments will, to some degree, fluctuate with the quality of service. For example, payment is reduced by a certain stated amount if particular deficiencies are found in the course of a joint inspection. Sometimes this approach has worked well – others have rapidly abandoned it. The key to its success seems to lie in the relationship between purchaser and supplier. Where both sides trust one another there is a better chance of it working than where there is a strongly adversarial relationship.

It is strongly advisable for the purchaser to have express rights of termination if the supplier is in breach of his duties. Absent an express clause, there will only be a right of termination if the failure of performance goes *to the root of the contract* – in other words, it is fundamental.

In addition to express rights of termination it is advisable to have a clause which allows the purchaser to terminate for a breach even if a similar breach has occurred in the past but on that occasion the purchaser chose not to terminate. This is to discourage a supplier who is in default from arguing that the other party, by previously ignoring a similar breach or breaches, has led him to believe that the right to terminate would never be exercised.

What has been considered so far is a service of a repetitive kind. There are some other considerations which apply to the *one-off* service such as the repair of a machine, the installation of a new central heating system or the upgrading of a computer system. With contracts of this kind it is advisable to specify expressly what the supplier must achieve under the contract and provide for a demonstration of this achievement. Thus if a computer is to be upgraded so that it will, for example, be able to process 1,000 documents within an hour, this should be stated and there should be an express term requiring the supplier to show this end has been reached by a monitored test.

A problem with some one-off services is when, during the course of performance, it becomes apparent that something is going wrong but the supplier is repeatedly reassuring: 'Don't worry we'll get there.' The trouble may arise where, for example, the supplier has a fixed period in which to perform, the clock is ticking but nothing seems to be happening. Again, the purchaser may be losing confidence but is promised that the supplier will, if necessary, put more people to work on the task or some other promise of this kind. This is not an easy situation – sometimes it is possible to solve the lack of progress by throwing in more resource but sometimes it is not.

One answer is that wherever appropriate the contract should have *milestones*, that is a requirement that certain stages in performance must be reached by certain dates. This is quite possible to do with, for example, a construction contract but less easy with a contract to upgrade a computer system. Where the supplier is seeking advance payments and these are geared to the achievement of milestones he has a powerful incentive to reach them. The contract should also provide remedies for failure to meet any milestone.

What if milestones are not feasible? In these circumstances it may be appropriate to have provisions which require the supplier to provide periodic reports on progress and to provide prompt notification of problems which may result in defects in the service provided or result in delay.

Failure to complete the service

If, due to some supervening event, the contract becomes frustrated, the legal effects of this are as described in Chapter 15.

If, however, the service supplier has rendered himself incapable of completing the service, or refuses to complete, then the position is different. This may be demonstrated by the following examples:

1. A and B enter into a contract in which B agrees to overhaul a machine at A's premises. B soon realises the task involved is greater than he expected. He refuses to do any more work. A is left with a dismantled machine.

   Here we have what is called an *entire contract* and B is not entitled to any part of his contract price even though, arguably, A has received some benefit in that the work has started. B is also liable for any damages.

2. C and D enter into a contract in which D agrees to carry out overhauls on *two* machines at C's premises. The consideration is expressed in the contract as £1,000 per machine. D completely overhauls one machine but refuses to come back and start work on the other.

The court would probably regard this as a *divisible contract* and C would be entitled to payment of £1,000. Of course, D would still be liable to B for damages for breach of contract in respect of the second machine.

3. E and F enter into a contract in which F agrees to overhaul a machine at E's premises. F carries out the work but when he claims payment E says the contract has not been completed because the specification required the machine to be finished with three coats of paint. E has only given it two coats.

    Here F is said to have *substantially performed* the contract and is entitled to the contract price less an appropriate deduction for the cost to E of applying the third coat of paint.

Late performance

Section 14 of the Supply of Goods and Services Act 1982 provides:

> Where, under a contract for the supply of a service by a supplier acting in the course of a business, the time for the service to be carried out is not fixed by the contract ... there is an implied term that the supplier will carry out the service within a reasonable time.

As with section 13, the term is only implied when the supplier is acting in the course of a business. It is not easy to find examples of someone who is performing services for a fee yet is not doing so in the course of a business. We know from cases involving the sale of goods that the expression *in the course of a business* applies to sales made by a supplier which are merely incidental to its business, such as the disposal of surplus vehicles or equipment. But with goods, obviously, there can be private sales.

The intention of the draftsman was presumably to exclude someone who performs a minor domestic repair for a friend in the expectation that he will be given some payment although his prime reason for agreeing to do the work was *as a favour*.

As ever, what is *reasonable* is a question of fact but if the provision of the service takes longer than anticipated it may still be regarded as reasonable if unforeseen circumstances are the cause of the delay. For example:

> X agrees to collect Y's goods on 1 June at 9:00 am and transport them by road. At the time the contract was made, five hours would have been regarded as a reasonable time for performance of the contract. After collection, X's driver is unexpectedly taken ill. X does his best to find another driver but inevitably there is a delay. The contract takes 10 hours to complete. X's performance as to time is judged in the light of what *actually* happened and there is no breach – this is illustrated by *Pantland Hick* v *Raymond & Reid* (see Appendix).
>
> Curiously, had the contract contained an express requirement that the contract be completed within five hours, X would be in breach unless he had the protection of an excusable delay clause (see Chapter 15).

Where the contract does contain a time for completion we are faced with the difficult question as to whether time is of the essence (see

Chapter 15) and *the best advice is that if the right to terminate for late performance is important to the purchaser then this should be provided for in the contract.*

Where no date for performance is included in the contract and time is running on, it is open to the customer to make *time of the essence* by a suitable notice. The notice should refer to the time which has elapsed, require the service to be performed by a named date and state that if this date is not met then the customer may terminate.

Subcontracting

It will be seen in Chapter 14 that in the absence of an express prohibition there is usually nothing to prevent a supplier of services from subcontracting the performance of them. Thought should be given to whether such a prohibition is required or, indeed, feasible.

Intellectual property rights

If the supplier and its personnel require access to intellectual property rights (IPR) of the purchaser (see Chapter 10) confidentiality agreements may be appropriate. Where the contract will or may result in the generation by the supplier of IPR further commentary will be found in Chapter 10.

Fidelity

If performance of the services requires the supplier's personnel to be on the purchaser's premises, consideration should be given to having a contractual requirement that the supplier obtains specified personal details from its personnel and makes them available to the purchaser.

A useful clause can be one that requires the supplier to ensure that all its personnel act honestly while on the purchaser's premises. It may be difficult for a supplier to police this but a breach of it will give the purchaser a remedy for breach of contract if it suffers a loss by reason of dishonesty.

Price

Constant pressures on budget make it tempting with service contracts, as with everything else, to opt for the lowest quotation. But service contracts in particular seem to attract a peculiar breed of bidder who will put in a price quotation far lower than that of anyone else. Experience has shown that where the work is given to 'a one man and a dog' organisation, which has bid a very low price, it is often unable to perform.

At pre-contract stage it is important to assess whether there is a real risk that such a bidder may have seriously underestimated the work involved. Before any contract award the question must be asked how serious the impact would be if the supplier fails to complete. It would be in breach of contract if it did so but, as ever, if it has few assets this would be of little help.

Accordingly, it may well be wise to require a potential supplier to provide not just a price quotation, but an estimate of the price of any materials it will use in performing the service and an estimate of man-hours the contract will require.

The purchaser's duty

In so far as is necessary, the purchaser of services has a duty to cooperate with the supplier to enable the latter to perform its duties. If the purchaser makes it impossible for the supplier to complete the work successfully, the supplier is entitled to be paid for the work it has done or would have done but for that lack of cooperation.

CHAPTER 10

Intellectual property rights

This chapter will examine what are intellectual property rights ('IPR'), give a short description of each of the main kinds, suggest when a purchaser needs to protect its IPR and when it should try to obtain the right to use a supplier's IPR.

The nature of IPR

IPR are those rights which protect ideas and the expression of those ideas. This is illustrated by the following example:

> X buys a book written by Y. X is, accordingly, the owner of that copy. As owner, he is free to do with it as he wishes; he can keep it, sell it, make a gift of it or even destroy it. What X *cannot* do is make copies of it; to do so would be a breach of Y's IPR, which in this case is copyright. Y, as the author,

owns the copyright in the text and as owner can prevent others from copying it.

In the same way that the owner of a car may sell or hire it to another person, so may the owner of IPR. The copyright in this book could be sold to someone else or *hired out* under a licence which would entitle the licensee to make copies while ownership would remain vested in the author.

But sometimes the position is not as clear-cut. For example, B devises a new manufacturing technique which drastically reduces the cost of producing a particular product. He decides not to try to seek a patent on this process but to stop his competitors using it informs only a few trusted employees of it. By keeping and using the technique in a confidential way B has a protectable IPR. It is confidential information and he has a legal remedy if someone tries to make use of it without his permission. However, it may be that a rival ('C') has replicated the same technique by his own efforts. It is not uncommon for competitors in the same industry each to reach similar results independently.

Provided C has not taken advantage of B's confidential information, there is nothing to stop C using the same manufacturing technique. B, by trying to rely on secrecy rather than obtaining a patent for his process, has taken a gamble which has not paid off.

The remainder of the chapter considers the main kinds of IPR.

Patents

A patent is a monopoly right to exploit an invention for a maximum period of 20 years. *Exploit* includes the right to manufacture, sell and also to prevent the import of any article which infringes the patent.

Patent law is territorial and so the inventor must decide in which countries patent registration needs to be obtained. There is nothing to stop someone else exploiting the patent in a territory where that invention has not been patented although it is now possible to obtain simultaneous registration in a number of European nations by applying to the European Patents Office. Steps are being taken to move to a common patent system in the European Union so that one registration will result in a Community Patent effective throughout the participating nations.

Patents in the United Kingdom are governed by the Patents Act 1977 which sets out the procedure for obtaining and maintaining a patent and gives guidance on which inventions are patentable.

A patent may relate to an artefact, a substance or a process. To obtain a patent, four hurdles have to be overcome:

- the invention must have *novelty* – if it is known about elsewhere then there is said to be *prior art*;

- it must contain *an inventive step* – that is, it must not be obvious;

- it must have *industrial application* – this means it can be applied industrially, thus a medicine may be patented but not a new surgical procedure;

- it must not be specifically excluded by the Patents Act – among the exclusions are computer software and inventions which may be protected by copyright.

An essential part of a patent application is the provision of a full description of it in a *patent specification*. This is a public document and at the end of the period of protection anyone is free to exploit the invention with the use of the patent specification.

Copyright

Copyright is the right of the creator of an original work to prevent people making copies.

There is no central registry of copyright; the volume is such that it would be impossible to maintain. Copyright legends are useful but not essential. The principal legislation governing copyright is the Copyright, Designs and Patents Act 1988.

In most cases, including copyright in documents, the period of copyright protection is the life of the author and 70 years from the author's death.

Copyright is concerned with unauthorised copying of a wide range of creative works. Obvious examples are books and newspapers but also included are recordings and films. Protection extends to sculpture, photographs, paintings and technical drawings.

For there to be an infringement the copying must be substantial (copying a title of a book or of a song is generally not enough) and there is a statutory defence of *fair dealing* which protects book reviewers and scholars who wish to copy short extracts.

Section 51 of the Copyright, Designs and Patents Act 1988 provides that to make a three-dimensional object by *reverse engineering* is *not* an infringement of the copyright in the original design data.

The exclusion in section 51 does not apply to an artistic work. Hence, copying an artistic work may be prevented and section 17 adds that in relation to an artistic work copying *includes the making of a copy in three dimensions of a two-dimensional work and the making of a copy in two dimensions of a three-dimensional work.*

The concept of copyright is not always an easy one to grasp but it helps to remember that there is no copyright in an idea – the copyright is in the *expression* of the idea.

Database right

The Copyright and Rights in Databases Regulations 1997 amend the Copyright etc. Act 1988 in respect of copyright in databases and they *also* create a new intellectual property right.

The 1988 Act provided that tables or compilations could be literary works and, subject to having originality, were protected by copyright. Originality under copyright law does not mean aesthetic creativity – *sweat of the brow* or *hard slog* are sufficient. *But* the Regulations now provide that the condition of originality in tables and compilations is only satisfied if the work constitutes the *author's own intellectual creation.* If not, the database may be protected by the database right if it can be shown that substantial investment in its creation has been made.

The period of protection is 15 years from creation or 15 years from substantial revision.

An important distinction between copyright protection in a database and database right is that mere unauthorised *use* of the latter may be a breach although such use may not amount to copying.

The Regulations define a database as:

> a collection of independent works, data or other material which
> (a) are arranged in a systematic or methodical way, and
> (b) are individually accessible by electronic or other means

Thus the inclusion of *other means* covers hard copies as well as electronic ones.

It would seem, for example, that a list of all restaurants in the United Kingdom, listed alphabetically by town, would be subject to database right not copyright. But any narrative concerning, for example, an inspector's experiences when visiting a restaurant would be copyright.

Irrespective of whether a database is the subject of copyright or database right it may be protectable by an action for breach of confidence (see below).

Registered design

In certain circumstances it is possible to register the visual aspect of a design at the Designs Registry and so protect it from imitation under the Registered Designs Act 1949 as amended by the 1988 Act. To qualify for registration the design of an article:

- must be *new*;

- must not be a method or principle of construction;

- must have features which in the finished article appeal to, and are judged by, the eye – often called *eye-appeal*;

- its shape or configuration must not be dictated by the function which the article has to perform;

- its shape or configuration must not be dependent upon the appearance of another article of which the article is intended by the author of the design to form an integral part.

The requirement that the design be new means *not available elsewhere*.

The requirement that the design must not be a method or principle of construction is difficult, but an example might be a piece of wooden furniture held together by distinctive wooden pegs.

The requirement of *eye-appeal* is also difficult. Potential purchasers may be influenced *both* by functionality as well as by appearance; this seems to be acceptable for registration. If the aesthetic aspect is not to be visible, for example the design is of a component which will be buried in another component, then registration is not possible.

Registration is not allowed if the design has been dictated by the need for the shape or configuration of the item to fit with another item or to match another item. The *must fit* and the *must match* exceptions prevent, for example, registration of motor body panels.

Subject to payment of fees a registered design may exist for 25 years. Protection of a registered design covers innocent infringement as well as deliberate copying.

Unregistered design right

This was introduced by the Copyright, Designs and Patents Act 1988 and is intended to protect for up to 15 years from creation (or 10 years from first marketing, whichever is less) original designs even though they may be purely functional and have *no eye-appeal.* The other conditions that apply to registered designs also apply and of particular importance are the *must fit* and *must match* exceptions.

To succeed in a claim for breach of unregistered design right it must be proved that there has been a *deliberate* copying and in this respect it differs from a registered design.

Impending changes to registered designs and to the unregistered design right

There is a firm intention to harmonise within the European Union the law relating to both these forms of IPR. It appears that some designs which cannot currently be protected will be capable of protection but that the *must fit* and *must match* exceptions will remain.

Trade marks

A trade mark is a distinctive symbol which causes the public to connect goods (or services) with the person or company that owns the mark. A logo is an obvious example, such as the red triangle of *Bass.* Another example is a made-up word: *OXO.*

Although a proprietor does not have to register a mark to protect it, registration at the Trade Mark Registry is advisable as it eliminates:

- the need to prove that its owner has used the mark;

- the need to prove that unauthorised use has caused confusion; and

- disputes as to whether or not the proprietor has used the mark in the same geographical region of the UK.

The Trade Marks Act 1994 extended the law by permitting the registration of sounds, smells and shapes which associate the product with its maker. However, protection is not available if the sound, smell or shape results from the nature of the goods themselves.

The protection afforded to a trade mark is without limitation of time subject to payment of fees. To succeed in a claim for infringement of a registered trade mark there is no need to show an intent to confuse or deceive.

There is now an EU system (under Council Regulation EC 40/94) known as the *Community Trade Mark* which allows simultaneous registration of a trade mark in some or all of the EU members. If a trade marked product or service is sold within the EU then this method of registration may well be appropriate.

Restrictions on passing off

An action for passing off is not the creation of statute but of case law. If someone is proved to be selling goods or services in a *get-up* which will confuse customers into thinking they are the established products or services of another, then they may be stopped. Confusion has to be shown. Search of a telephone directory is likely

---

to find people with the surname of 'Marks' and people with the surname 'Spencer'. If a person in each group agreed with the other to open a clothing store in both names, it is likely that an established chain store would bring a passing off action!

An action for passing off is also appropriate if the *get-up* falsely suggests the goods are produced in a particular geographical region, for example champagne.

The extension of the definition of trade marks in the 1994 Act to allow registration of sounds, smells and shapes has reduced the number of passing off actions.

Confidential information

Within this category of IPR lies a wide spectrum of different classes of information.

At one extreme is the kind of material which everyone can recognise as being of enormous value which would be greatly diminished if it fell into the wrong hands. Formulae, production processes and other things which give their possessor a competitive advantage are good examples. These are often referred to as *trade secrets* and in high technology organisations are often called the *crown jewels*. Although the latter is a little emotional it does stress the great value of such knowledge.

In the middle of the spectrum we find the sort of information that the holder desires to keep confidential because disclosure would be disadvantageous, but whose confidentiality may not necessarily be obvious to someone else. A lot of material that a prospective supplier might put into a tender is likely to be in this area such as prices and delivery dates. In the case of a purchaser it may be important to keep confidential the intention to purchase particular goods or services because such information could be of value to a competitor.

Then, at the far end of the spectrum, we find information that an organisation would *like* to protect. Many an employer has been dismayed when someone it has trained intensively for a long time leaves and goes to another job – 'We taught him everything he knows and this is how he repays us.'

As far as trade secrets are concerned, if these unlawfully fall into the hands of a third party then as a basic proposition, use or further disclosure is unlawful even in the absence of any express promise not to disclose. It will be seen later that it is best not to leave things to chance and disclosure of such material should best be made on the strength of an express, written promise by the recipient to maintain confidentiality.

Turning to the second category (that which is valuable to its holder but whose value is not apparent to everybody) this kind of information may only be protected if it is the subject of a confidentiality agreement or, failing that, a legend (see below).

The third category cannot be restricted. There is ample case law on the inability to prevent an ex-employee taking his or her skills and knowledge to a new job.

The purchaser and confidential information

Often, a would-be purchaser is unable to obtain a meaningful quotation without disclosing to potential suppliers confidential information of a technical and/or commercial nature.

As a minimum if such information is to be disclosed when seeking a quotation/tender, the request for quotation/request for tender should contain a legend upon the front page along the following lines:

> *This document contains information which [Purchaser] regards as being of a technical and/or commercially confidential nature and also the subject of copyright. Accordingly it shall not be disclosed or copied, in whole or in part, to any third party, without the prior written permission of [Purchaser]. Further, the recipient shall not use the information, nor disclose it to any of its employees, except to the extent necessary to enable the preparation of the documentation for which it has been provided.*

In certain circumstances, either when seeking a quotation/tender or to enable the contract to be performed, a separate non-disclosure agreement should be signed or appropriate clauses should be included in the purchase contract. The following should be considered for inclusion:

All written information marked with a legend indicating that the disclosing party (DP) regards it as technically or commercially confidential shall be treated by the receiving party (RP) as follows:

- No disclosure to any third party without DP's prior written consent.

- No disclosure to any employee of RP except to the extent necessary to enable the quotation/tender to be prepared or the contract performed.

- Employees to whom disclosure is to be made shall sign a short-form agreement acknowledging that they will be handling confidential information belonging to the DP and undertaking that they will not make disclosures to any third party. (The DP shall be entitled to have copies of these signed agreements.)

- At all times the confidential information to be kept in a secure fashion.

- At the end of the quotation/tendering process or performance of contract, RP, if requested, to destroy or return to DP (as specified by DP) all such information and any copies.

- No use to be made by RP of the information except for the purpose for which it was supplied by the DP.

- Any computer software, source codes, logic and similar provided by DP to be treated as confidential even if not marked with a legend. (This recognises the difficulty of placing legends on electronically held information.)

- Any oral information provided by DP to be treated as confidential if RP is informed in writing that such oral information is to be treated by RP as if it were written confidential information.

The golden rule is that where the information is of major importance, or is unlikely to cease to be of importance in the long term, it should not be left to be protected merely by a legend. Such information should only be disclosed after the receiving party has signed a properly drafted agreement.

A purchaser's rights in a supplier's IPR

In the absence of an express agreement to the contrary, it is probable that a supplier (unlike an employee of the purchaser) which uses its existing IPR or develops new IPR in the course of performing a contract retains ownership of it to the exclusion of the purchaser, for example:

- a photographer commissioned to take photographs;

- an engineering company which designs a new component and then sells those components to the purchaser.

Whenever *new* IPR is likely to be generated by a supplier in the course of performing a contract the purchaser needs to consider what the IPR position will be if that supplier becomes unable or unwilling to supply production units (or, indeed, becomes too expensive). In any of these events the purchaser may need to source production requirements in-house or to find another supplier. What IPR rights the purchaser is able to get will be a matter for negotiation but the following should be considered:

- The purchaser should be given sufficient data relating to the IPR (including updates) to enable it to source elsewhere.

- If the supplier is unable or unwilling to perform follow-on production contracts at similar prices/delivery schedules to those within the present contract, the purchaser shall be entitled to make use of such supplier's IPR (whether by making it available to another supplier or by using it in-house as is necessary).

- No licence fee, royalty or other payment shall be due to the original supplier for the use of IPR as described above.

Special considerations apply to software designed or developed by a supplier and then licensed to a purchaser. There is always the fear that, in the future, the software house may be unable/unwilling to supply vital updates. The answer is an escrow agreement whereby source codes and other logic necessary to modify the software are held in a central repository managed by a third party, which will release it to the purchaser if the supplier can no longer provide these updates. The problem is if the software house fails to provide the third party with any updates of the source code and logic.

In so far as a supplier uses its *existing* IPR in the performance of a contract it is harder to negotiate free of charge rights for the purchaser to use it in the circumstances described earlier. Accordingly, consideration should be given to obtaining a licence which entitles the purchaser to use existing IPR in exchange for a licence fee and/or royalty.

Before attempting to negotiate rights to use a supplier's existing or arising IPR the question should be asked: could we *actually* use it? It may be that the purchaser itself or other suppliers will not have the general skill, know-how, equipment or other resources to make its use a practical proposition. If this is so then there seems little point in demanding something which has no utility.

In so far as suggestions have been made in this chapter on protecting the purchaser's position it has to be remembered that they are no more than suggestions. Every transaction needs to be looked at individually.

CHAPTER 11

Exemption clauses and the
Unfair Contract Terms Act 1977

Exemption clauses

An exemption clause is one which either restricts or excludes altogether the liability a party would otherwise have for a breach of contract or for other actionable conduct such as negligence. A clause may restrict liability by, for example, specifying a maximum financial limit on the compensation payable or by providing that the party at fault ceases to have any liability after a certain period of time. Sometimes the wording of them can be subtle:

> *Any defect discovered in the goods more than six months from its first operation by the buyer shall be deemed to result from fair wear and tear and not from any defect in the quality of the goods.*

If the seller was allowed to rely on such a clause it would thus limit its liability to six months for a breach of the statutory implied condition that the goods should be of satisfactory quality. Section 14(2) of the Sale of Goods Act 1979, which implies the term as to satisfactory quality, imposes no such time limit.

An interesting point arises with durability. If, instead of this clause, there had been included as part of the description the following statement about the durability of the goods then, unless it was a sham, it would probably not be treated as an exemption clause:

> *The goods are designed to have a short operating life and should not be used for a period longer than six months.*

Exemption clauses have been tolerated in the law of contract not least because of the principle that it is for the parties to make their own bargain. To say they have been *tolerated* is not to say the courts have ever liked them or encouraged them. In construing them they have tended to apply the *contra proferentem* rule – that is, any possible ambiguity is resolved contrary to the interest of the party seeking to rely upon the clause. That said, the position at common law is that if an exemption clause is clear then it will have the effect of relieving a party from a liability it would otherwise have.

It is now necessary to examine the extent to which the Unfair Contract Terms Act 1977 has eroded the common law position. For the remainder of this chapter the statute is referred to as 'UCTA' and all references to sections are to sections of UCTA unless otherwise stated.

UCTA treats exemption clauses much more strictly where a party to a contract *deals as consumer*. For a party to deal as consumer section 12(1) imposes these requirements:

(a) he neither makes the contract in the course of a business nor holds himself out as doing so; and

(b) the other party does make the contract in the course of a business; and

(c) ... the goods passing under or in pursuance of the contract are of a type ordinarily supplied for private use or consumption.

From the above it would thus seem that the consumer provisions of UCTA have no relevance to purchases made by individuals in the course of their employment by companies or other organisations. But, surprisingly, the Court of Appeal in 1987 decided a company could be a consumer in a case called *R & B Customs Brokers* v *UDT*. In this case R & B, a small company owned by a husband and wife, bought a Colt Shogun for both business and private use. The purchase was in the name of the company. The car roof leaked and in the end the purchaser rejected the car.

R & B sued the finance company with whom it had a contract. The case largely turned on whether the finance company could rely on an exemption clause which purported to exclude it from liability for a breach of section 14 of the Sale of Goods Act 1979. If the plaintiff had dealt as consumer, the exemption clause would have been void under UCTA. If the plaintiff bought the car other than as a consumer, the exemption could have been effective if it satisfied the requirement of reasonableness (see later).

Surprisingly, in the view of many lawyers, the court ruled that R & B had dealt as consumer and the exemption clause was void. The court said that over the years R & B had traded it had only bought two or three cars and so it was not buying in the course of its business as shipping brokers.

Even if R & B could not be said to have bought in the course of business it would seem to have *held itself out* as doing so. The court, however, placed little weight on the fact that the purchase was in the name of the company, that the contract described its business as shipping brokers and that it also contained details of the number of years it had traded and the names of the directors.

This decision was the cause of some difficulty to another Court of Appeal which chose not to apply it in a more recent case called *Stevenson* v *Rogers* and it remains to be seen whether, in the future, it will be overruled. In *Stevenson* v *Rogers* it was held that a fisherman who disposed of his fishing boat so that he could buy another was acting in the course of a business.

It can safely be stated that very few commercial purchases will ever allow an interpretation that the purchaser was dealing as consumer. Indeed, even in the R & B case, the court said that a professional man who buys a carpet for his office or an employer which buys a company car for the use of an employee is not dealing as consumer. *Professional purchasers should* never *assume that they have the protection given to consumers under UCTA.*

From now on this chapter will concentrate on contracts where the purchaser does not deal as consumer.

Section 1(3) provides that, with a few exceptions, UCTA only applies where the party seeking to shelter behind an exemption clause or notice has a *business liability* which is defined as:

> ... liability for breach of obligations or duties arising –
>
> (a) from things done or to be done by a person in the course of a business (whether his own business or another's); or
>
> (b) from the occupation of premises used for business purposes of the occupier ...

Excluding liability for negligence

Section 2 deals both with contract terms which attempt to restrict or exclude liability for negligence and with notices which are not contractual.

An example of the former is a contract term which seeks to exclude or restrict liability for a breach of the term implied by section 13 of the Supply of Goods and Services Act 1982 that in a contract for the supply of a service the supplier will carry out the service with reasonable care and skill.

The relevance of including non-contractual notices in section 2 may be illustrated by the following:

> A takes B to the zoo and A buys the tickets. At the entrance is a sign stating that the zoo shall have no liability for injury to members of the public howsoever caused and entry to the zoo is subject to acceptance of the terms of the notice. B, of course, has no contract with the zoo. He is savaged by a lion

which escapes due to the zoo's negligence. Such a notice is controlled by section 2(1) which provides:

'A person cannot by reference to any contract term or to a notice given to persons generally or to particular persons exclude or restrict his liability for death or personal injury resulting from negligence.'

Accordingly, any such notice is void.

Other liability arising from negligence (such as damage to property or loss of profit) is capable of exclusion or restriction by a contract term or notice ... *in so far as the term or notice satisfies the requirement of reasonableness* (section 2(2)).

The need to satisfy this requirement of reasonableness features in various places in UCTA and will be discussed in more detail later.

Exemption clauses in general

Section 3 contains a blanket provision that *any* term in a contract which attempts to restrict or exclude liability for *any* breach has to satisfy the requirement of reasonableness if:

- one of the parties to it deals as consumer; or

- the contract is on one party's *standard terms of business*.

In the first case the party who is not the consumer and in the second case the party whose standard terms of business form the contract can only rely on the clause if the requirement of reasonableness is satisfied.

Section 3 applies not only to clauses which attempt to restrict or exclude liability but also to contract terms which allow the defendant:

(i) to render a contractual performance substantially different from that which was reasonably expected of him, or

(ii) in respect of the whole or any part of his contractual obligation, to render no performance at all ...

(section 3(2)(b))

An example of a term contemplated by (i) is one which allowed a seller to substitute different goods from those described in the contract. If the contract was for a table made of rosewood and that delivered was of chipboard, the seller would have to justify the reasonableness of such a term.

An example of a term contemplated by (ii) is one which allows the seller a unilateral right to terminate the contract.

What is meant by *standard terms of business*? The term is used to take out of the ambit of section 3 any contract where the terms have been specifically negotiated by the parties. It would seem the standard form contracts drawn up by professional and trade associations for use by their members would be within the ambit.

Some guidance may also be found in the leading case of *St Albans City and District Council* v *International Computers Ltd* where it was held that standard terms of business remain so, even though not all of the terms have been fixed by the supplier. There may be individual negotiation of such matters as price and delivery.

The rest of the document will be treated as standard terms of business.

Exemption clauses relating to title and similar

It is fundamental that where the parties to a contract intend that title (ownership) in goods shall pass from one to another, the buyer or transferee shall actually become the owner of the goods. Section 6(1) recognises the importance of this principle by *entrenching* section 12 of the Sale of Goods Act (the seller shall transfer title to the goods etc.) so that liability for breach cannot be excluded or restricted in the contract.

This inability to restrict or exclude section 12 of the 1979 Act is applicable to any contract whether or not the buyer deals as a consumer and whether or not the contract is on the seller's standard terms. What is more, these prohibitions even apply where the sale has not been made in the course of a business (section 6(4)).

Section 7(3A) was added by amendment in 1982. It provides that where there is a contract involving the transfer of title in goods and which is governed by the Supply of Goods and Services Act 1982, then the terms implied by that Act relating to the transferor's liability for failure to transfer good title etc. '... cannot be excluded or restricted by references to any such term.'

Section 7(4) provides:

> Liability in respect of –
> (a) the right to transfer ownership of the goods, or give possession; or

(b) the assurance of quiet possession to a person taking goods in pursuance of the contract,

cannot (in a case to which subsection (3A) does not apply) be excluded or restricted by reference to any such term except in so far as the term satisfies the requirement of reasonableness.

Given that section 7(4) does not apply to:

- contracts for the sale of goods and contracts of hire purchase which are subject to section 6(1)

- contracts involving the transfer of ownership to goods which are subject to subsection 3A

it is difficult to think of examples of other contracts which do result in the transfer of ownership but are not governed by section 6(1) or 7(3A).

Section 7(4), however, also deals with the right to transfer possession – it implies terms into a contract for hire that the bailor has:

- a right to give possession to the bailee; and

- a duty to allow the bailee quiet possession of the goods subject only to charges or encumbrances disclosed or known to the bailor before the contract.

The effect of section 7(4) is that any attempt to restrict or exclude the above duties of a bailor in a contract of hire is subject to the requirement of reasonableness.

Exemption clauses relating to correspondence of goods with description or sample or as to quality or fitness for purpose

In contracts for the sale of goods these are the conditions implied by sections 13 to 15 of the Sale of Goods Act 1979 – the seller's implied undertakings as to conformity of goods with description or sample or as to their quality or fitness for a particular purpose.

Section 6(2) provides where the buyer deals as consumer that any clause attempting to restrict or exclude liability is void. *In all other cases such a clause must meet the requirement of reasonableness* (section 6(3)). This prohibition extends even where the seller is not acting in the course of a business (section 6(4)).

In contracts which are *not* subject to the Sale of Goods Act but *are* contracts for the transfer or hire of goods, similar terms to those implied by sections 13, 14 and 15 above are implied by sections 3, 4 and 5 (in the case of transfer) and sections 8, 9 and 10 (in the case of hire) of the Supply of Goods and Services Act 1982. Where the transferee or bailee in such a contract deals as consumer any clause attempting to restrict or exclude liability for breach is void and in any other case such a clause must meet the requirement of reasonableness provided the transferor or bailor is acting in the course of a business. This latter proviso thus contrasts clauses 6 and 7.

The requirement of reasonableness

The requirement of reasonableness in relation to a contract term:

> ... is that the term shall have been a fair and reasonable one to be included having regard to the circumstances which

were, or ought reasonably to have been, known to or in the contemplation of the parties when the contract was made.

(section 11(1))

Similar, general words are used to describe how reasonableness shall be assessed in a non-contractual notice which purports to restrict or exclude liability for negligence.

Section 11(2) provides that in assessing reasonableness, particular regard shall be had to Schedule 2. This schedule, which is entitled *Guidelines for Application of Reasonableness Test*, specifies five matters which should be considered:

- *The strengths of the bargaining positions of the parties.* Was, for example, the customer able to get similar goods elsewhere? Or was the supplier in a monopoly position?

- *Whether the customer received an inducement to agree to the term.* Was there a set of express terms which gave the customer strong remedies against the supplier in return for excluding the supplier's liability for breach of the implied condition that the goods should be of satisfactory quality? Could the goods or services have been obtained from someone else on similar terms, except for the excluding clause?

- *Whether the customer knew or ought reasonably to have known of the term.* Did it appear prominently in the contract or was it hidden away in the small print?

- *Where the term excludes or restricts any relevant liability if some condition was not complied with.* Was it reasonable at the time the contract was made to expect compliance with that condition? For example, if the supplier's liability for defects in the goods was subject to those defects being brought to its attention within 48 hours of their discovery by the customer, might there have been foreseen circumstances which would cause the customer to wait for a longer period?

- *Whether the goods were manufactured, processed or adapted to the special order of the customer.* It seems this guideline is intended to apply to circumstances where the seller has agreed to vary a standard product to meet the purchaser's particular requirements. An example would be where the supplier has to render waterproof a product which otherwise would not be waterproof. It is difficult to tell whether, in these circumstances, the inclusion of an exemption clause should be more or less likely to be regarded as reasonable. It is arguable either way.

Section 11(5) provides that where a contract term or notice is challenged on the basis of reasonableness *it is for those claiming that the contract term or notice satisfies the requirement of reasonableness to show that it does.*

International supply contracts

Section 26 provides that where there is a contract involving the sale or other transfer of ownership or possession of goods, and that contract has an international element, those parts of UCTA which govern the use of exemption clauses shall not apply.

The contract has an international element if:

- The parties have their places of business in territories of different states. The Channel Islands and the Isle of Man are regarded as different states from the rest of the United Kingdom.

- England, Wales, Scotland and Northern Ireland are all regarded as the same state. Thus if a contract is between an English company and a Scottish company it is necessary to find out if the contract is subject to English or to Scots law. If the former, the relevant part of UCTA is Part I and if the latter, Part II, which applies to Scotland.

Section 26 only takes a contract outside the control of UCTA if:

- the goods at the time the contract is made will need to be carried from the territory of one state to the territory of another state or are in the course of such carriage; or

- the offer and the acceptance have taken place in different states; or

- the offer and acceptance have taken place in the same state but the goods are to be delivered in the territory of another state.

Section 26 only applies to international supply contracts where either title or possession of goods is transferred. Accordingly, in so far as a contract is for the supply of services and is subject to the law of any part of the United Kingdom, then section 2 (exclusion or restriction of liability for negligence) will apply even though it has an international element.

Choice of law

Section 27(1) provides that where the law applicable to a contract is that of any part of the United Kingdom only by express choice of the parties (and would have been the law of some country outside the United Kingdom but for that choice) sections 2 to 7 (restrictions on exemption clauses in England and Wales and Northern Ireland) and sections 16 to 21 (restrictions on exemption clauses in Scotland) shall not apply as part of the law applicable to the contract.

Section 27(2) deals with the converse situations where either the governing law of the contract is expressed to be that of a territory outside the United Kingdom and:

- the choice of law was intended mainly or wholly to prevent the application of UCTA; or

- one of the parties dealt as consumer and was at the time of the contract habitually resident in the United Kingdom and the contract was made there.

In both these cases the UCTA controls on exemption clauses apply. For further guidance on choice of law in contracts see Chapter 19.

Purchasers seeking to rely on exemption clauses

In many places in this chapter the assumption has been made that it is the supplier who will seek to rely on an exemption clause. This will normally be the case as most express and implied duties fall upon the supplier. In most contracts the purchaser only has two duties: to allow the performance of the service or the delivery of the goods contracted for, and to pay the contract price. But UCTA *could* be a supplier's weapon.

Under section 13(1) a clause making a contract liability or its enforcement *subject to restrictive or onerous conditions* is subject to the UCTA provisions. Thus if a purchaser's standard terms attempted to exclude its liability for not accepting delivery of goods imposed by section 27 of the Sale of Goods Act 1979 (see Chapter 7) such a term would be open to challenge on the basis of reasonableness.

Other restrictions on exemption clauses

UCTA is not the only statute dealing with the subject.

Section 3 of the Misrepresentation Act 1967 (which was amended by UCTA) subjects clauses which attempt to restrict or exclude any liability or remedy for a pre-contract misrepresentation to the requirement of reasonableness. Accordingly, a clause (often called *an entire agreement clause*) which purports to exclude any liability for misrepresentation by saying no representation has been made is not watertight if, in fact, misrepresentations have been made.

A further example of a restriction on exemption clauses will be found in the Late Payment of Commercial Debts (Interest) Act 1998 (see Chapter 16).

The value of UCTA in contract negotiations

Often the most heated part of a contract negotiation comes when the supplier attempts to introduce and justify exemption clauses. In so far as the proposed term is one which is subject to the requirement of reasonableness it may be useful to tell the supplier's representatives that even if the clause is accepted then any attempt to rely on it will be subject to challenge. It might also be worth suggesting that, if forced to accept it, then contract signature will coincide with a letter indicating that the term is regarded as unreasonable – and why.

The following quotation from *St Albans City and District Council* v *International Computers Ltd* might, if pointed out, also lead the supplier to question the value of the clause:

> I do not think it unreasonable that he who stands to make the profit should carry the risk.

CHAPTER 12

Privity of contract and the Contracts (Rights of Third Parties) Act 1999

Privity

The doctrine of privity of contract is that only the contracting parties may enforce the rights and suffer the liabilities under it. The origins of the doctrine have been widely debated and some eminent authorities have even questioned its validity. However, in 1968 in *Beswick* v *Beswick*, the House of Lords reaffirmed that the privity doctrine was good law. The facts of this celebrated case provide a good illustration of the injustice privity may cause:

> *Mr Beswick was a coal merchant. The time came for him to retire. He transferred his business to his nephew in return for a*

---

weekly income for the rest of his life and a weekly payment of £5 to his widow after his death. When he died, the nephew broke his undertaking and only ever made one payment to Mrs Beswick.

The House of Lords held that Mrs Beswick could not sue in her personal capacity as the breach was of a contract to which she was not a party. Justice was achieved in another way: she had also sued as *administratrix* of her late husband's estate and in that capacity obtained an order for specific performance of the nephew's obligation to his uncle to pay the weekly sum (see Chapter 17).

Privity is perfectly sensible in so far as it prevents a contract between A and B imposing a *duty* upon C but where A and B intend that *a benefit* should be conferred on C, the doctrine may have the effect of defeating the intention of the contract parties at the time the contract was made.

There are a number of exceptions to the privity rule – some statutory and some common law.

Under section 151 of the Road Traffic Act 1988 it is thus possible for a road traffic victim who has obtained a judgment against an insured driver, to enforce the judgment directly against the insurer.

A common law exception allows a building developer to sue a building contractor for poor workmanship even though at the time the action is brought the former has disposed of the property and so has not suffered any loss. In these circumstances the developer is deemed to hold the contractor's obligation to use reasonable care and skill in trust for the current owner of the property. Damages recovered by the developer are also held in trust for the person who actually suffers the loss.

Another device for steering around the problem is by *agency*, which may be illustrated as follows:

> *Black plc* has three subsidiaries – *Blue Ltd*, *White Ltd* and *Red Ltd*. All four companies occupy different buildings and carry on different activities.
>
> *Black* decides to buy new computer equipment for all four of them and makes the contract of purchase in its own name and as agent for *Blue*, *White* and *Red*. The three subsidiaries are parties to the contract and, as such, may sue and be sued on it.
>
> If the computer supplied to *Blue* is defective and causes that company a loss of profit *Blue* is able to sue the supplier for it. If only *Black* had been able to sue the measure of damages might have been considerably lower.

The disadvantage of using agency in this way is that the contract drafting is complicated. Further, it is not available as an option if Black wishes to buy on behalf of a party not in existence at the time the contract is made.

Privity has become a messy doctrine resulting in frequent doubt as to whether it applies to a particular promise. Furthermore, the inability in most cases to confer enforceable rights on third parties has made English law inconsistent with the laws of most countries which apply common law and also with the laws of most members of the European Union.

The Contracts (Rights of Third Parties) Act 1999

This legislation gives to contracting parties an ability to avoid the difficulties that privity can cause. It is also a response to the judges who, over the years, have said it is for Parliament to provide relief from its injustice.

The Act is undoubtedly capable of being a great help although, as will be seen, some of its provisions are puzzling.

Section 1(1):

> Subject to the provisions of this Act, a person who is not a party to a contract (a 'third party') may in his own right, enforce a term of the contract if –
>
> (a) the contract expressly provides that he may, or
>
> (b) ... the term purports to confer a benefit on him.

To deal with the problem posed earlier, and to take advantage of the 1999 legislation, Black plc should negotiate into the contract words along the following lines:

> *The terms of this contract which are enforceable by Black plc may also be enforced by any of the following: Blue Ltd, White Ltd and Red Ltd.*

A similar result could be achieved with suitable words which make clear that the goods to be provided by the supplier were for the benefit of Black plc, Blue Ltd, White Ltd and Red Ltd.

It is likely, however, that the first approach suggested will be easier to express in writing. Furthermore, section 1(1)(b) is subject to section 1(2) which provides that 1(1)(b) does not apply:

... if on a proper construction of the contract it appears that the parties did not intend the term to be enforceable by the third party.

Those words must, at least, raise some doubt about how reliance on section 1(1)(b) is to be achieved in drafting. As the statute only came fully into effect on 11 May 2000, there is no body of case law to provide guidance.

Section 1(3) provides:

The third party must be clearly identified in the contract by name, as a member of a class or as answering a particular description but need not be in existence when the contract is entered into.

For a company like Black plc, this last part of section 1(3) is helpful as its contract could identify the third parties as '... any company which is, or becomes in the future, a subsidiary of Black plc'.

Section 2(1) provides:

Subject to the provisions of this section, where a third party has a right under section 1 to enforce a term of the contract, the parties to the contract may not, by agreement, rescind the contract, or vary it in such a way as to extinguish or alter his entitlement under that right, without his consent, if –

(a) the third party has communicated his assent to the term to the promisor,

(b) the promisor is aware that the third party has relied on the term, or

(c) the promisor can reasonably be expected to have foreseen that the third party would rely on the term and the third party has in fact relied upon it.

In November 1999 the Lord Chancellor's Department published explanatory notes which dealt with section 2(1) as follows:

> ... where a third party has a right under section 1, the contracting parties may not, by agreement, rescind or vary the contract in a way which affects the third party's right without his consent.

But section 2(1) says more than this: the right of the third party not to have his right removed or varied is subject to meeting the criteria of either paragraphs (a) or (b) or (c) of section 2(1).

It is worth considering the position of a latter-day Mrs Beswick if her husband and his nephew, after making the agreement, had then agreed to reduce or cancel her weekly payment. Could she still claim the original payment?

If she had been unaware of the term in the agreement (stranger things happen between husbands and wives) then she could not. She could not have assented to or relied upon a benefit she did not know of at the time of the contract amendment.

If she *had* been aware of the original agreement it is a little strange to expect her to have *communicated her assent* to the nephew as required under section 2(1)(a). *Assent* is another word for *consent* or *agreement* and its use does not fit in neatly with the principle of a gratuitous benefit to her. If someone may assent to something then, by implication, they have a power to refuse.

As far as (b) and (c) are concerned, it is easier to imagine circumstances where the lady may be said to have relied upon the term and where the nephew is aware of, or reasonably could have foreseen, that reliance. She may, for example, during her husband's life have made less provision for her old age than she would otherwise have done had she not had the expectation of the £5 a week.

If the group purchasing example, described earlier, is subjected to the same analysis, it is difficult to envisage the three subsidiaries, Blue, White or Red, communicating their assent to the supplier's promises or being reliant upon the term in circumstances where the supplier either knows of that reliance or could reasonably foresee it.

Paragraphs (a), (b) and (c) of section 2(1) are dealt with by the Law Commission in its 1996 Report which led to the legislation. It referred to (a), (b) and (c) as *crystallisations* of the right of the third party to refuse to allow his rights under the contract to be removed or altered. In advocating the principle of crystallisation in the UK legislation, the Commission followed Commonwealth legislation on the same subject but has given very little guidance on how it should be handled.

Section 2(3) allows the contracting parties to prevent or vary crystallisation under subsection (1):

> Subsection (1) is subject to any express term of the contract under which –
>
> (a) the parties to the contract may by agreement rescind or vary the contract without the consent of the third party, or

(b) the consent of the third party is required in circumstances specified in the contract instead of those set out in subsection (1)(a) to (c).

In the case of commercial purchasers who are buying for subsidiaries, it is probably safer to avoid crystallisation and to have in the contract words which allow the contracting parties to rescind or vary the contract without the consent of the third party. Circumstances change – subsidiary companies are sold to new owners and there may be good reasons in the future for divesting a third party of such rights.

Elsewhere, the Act provides that where a third party seeks to enforce a term of a contract, the promisor has all the defences and rights that would have been available had the claim been made by the other party to the contract. In other words the promisor is not put in a worse position if he is sued by the third party.

If the contract contains an arbitration clause then the third party has to enforce the term by arbitration rather than through the ordinary courts.

In one respect a promisor faced with a claim made by a third party may be in a better position than if faced with a claim by the other party. It will be recalled from Chapter 11 that section 2 of the Unfair Contract Terms Act 1977 provides:

(1) A person cannot by reference to any contract term or to a notice given to persons generally or to particular persons exclude or restrict his liability for death or personal injury resulting from negligence.

(2) In the case of other loss or damage, a person cannot so exclude or restrict his liability for negligence except in so far as the term or notice satisfies the requirement of reasonableness.

Section 7(2) of the 1999 Act provides that where a third party sues for a breach of a contract term and that breach is the failure of the promissor to use reasonable care and skill, the third party does not have the benefit of section 2(2) of UCTA. The effect of this is that where a third party sues for breach of such a term then, provided the claim is not in respect of death or personal injury, an exemption clause which protects the promisor is not subject to the requirement of reasonableness. If the claim was made by the other contracting party the exemption clause would have been subject to the requirement of reasonableness.

So far, this chapter has looked at the Contracts (Rights of Third Parties) Act as providing a third party with rights to sue on it. There is, however, at section 1(6) a short but rather important provision:

Where a term of a contract excludes or limits liability in relation to any matter references in this Act to the third party enforcing the term shall be construed as references to his availing himself of the exclusion or limitation.

Let us consider the following example:

P is a company which has entered into a contract with Q to build Q a new factory and equip it.

P is to buy all the equipment and materials and to perform all the services. There are contract provisions requiring P to use R and S as subcontractors. R and S are other subsidiary companies within the same group as P.

The contract between P and Q contains the following clause: '... neither P, R or S shall have any liability for negligence to Q in respect of any loss caused to Q by reason of any defects in any goods or services used in the performance in this contract.'

In respect of damage (other than personal injury or death) and subject to the requirement of reasonableness, these words are capable of excluding the liability of P, but in the absence of section 1(6) R or S could not have relied upon them as the exclusion language was contained in a contract to which neither was a party.

Accordingly, although most of the Act is intended to give a third party a *sword*, section 1(6) may give it a *shield*.

The extent to which purchasers will want to rely upon the Act remains to be seen, as will the extent to which purchasers will prefer to exclude it. If it is to be excluded then, subject to the structure of the contract, the following may be suitable:

> *No term of this contract shall be enforceable by any third party and the provisions of the Contracts (Rights of Third Parties) Act 1999 are hereby excluded.*

If the Act is excluded the common law doctrine of privity will apply together with the exceptions to it. In so far as the exceptions to the doctrine are based upon the intention of the parties to provide a benefit to a third party, the suggested words of exclusion above are likely to negate that intention.

CHAPTER 13

Amendment and novation

of contracts

These terms are often confused.

Amendment of a contract arises where the parties agree to a variation of a term or terms of it so that performance will be in some respect different from that originally provided.

The parties are always free to make an amendment provided each of them assumes a new duty under the contract. The following is a simple example:

> The contract requires A to supply *white* office furniture to B. Before delivery A asks B if instead of white furniture *black* furniture could be supplied. B agrees.

From that time A's new duty is to deliver black furniture in accordance with the contract (as amended) and B's new duty is to accept delivery of black furniture. Each party has assumed a different obligation to the other party and so each has provided consideration for the amendment.

The requirement for consideration raises a problem where the amendment consists merely of one party having its obligation reduced or relaxed with no benefit accruing to the other. The following is an example:

> X agrees to paint Y's house in consideration for a payment of £1,000. At some stage Y tells X he can no longer afford the amount. They agree that the price shall be reduced to £750. Here, X cannot be said to receive any consideration for accepting a lesser sum. There is considerable legal doubt as to the effectiveness of this amendment.

There are three ways to make it effective:

- Firstly, if Y provides consideration by *another* amendment to the contract. An example would be if in return for X agreeing to the price reduction Y agrees to X starting work later than that provided for in the contract. Or perhaps that Y pays some of the price earlier than he was bound to do under the contract.

- Secondly, if X, *by deed*, agrees to accept the lesser price as full consideration for the work this would solve the problem – a promise contained in a deed does not need consideration to be enforceable.

- Thirdly, there is the doctrine of *promissory estoppel* which will forever be associated with the judgement of the late Lord

Denning in a case called *Central London Property Trust* v *High Trees House Ltd.* Here, the landlord let a block of flats in London to a tenant on a long lease at an annual rent of £2,500 per year. Then came the Second World War and the flats in London became hard to let. The landlord promised to reduce the rent by half.

Lord Denning took the view that in the appropriate circumstances (that is, if the promise was unambiguous, intended by the person making it to affect the contract and the promise has been relied on by the other party) then the person to whom the promise is made is entitled to rely upon it.

The subject of promissory estoppel has been the subject of academic debate ever since but as far as the amendment of contracts is concerned it seems to be no more than waiver of a right. In commercial life, waivers are granted all the time and are accepted by the courts. Here is an example:

> A contract between B and C is for the performance of services by B which are to be completed by 1 June. Before that date arrives, B goes *cap in hand* to C and asks for a further month. C, although displeased, grants B that extension.

C has waived his right to have performance completed by 1 June and cannot, during the extension period, claim B is in breach. What is open to C to do, if he fears that B will not finish by July, is to put B on notice that if the work is not completed by that later time he will treat B's failure to complete as a repudiation of the contract and treat it as discharged.

It is certainly open to C to provide this notice at or near the time he granted the waiver. If, however, he provided it near to the end of the month of June this might well not be regarded as reasonable. There will be further discussion of notices of this kind in Chapter 15.

An oral amendment to a written contract is legally effective although oral amendments are usually unwise. Where, by law, a contract has to be in writing then an amendment to it must also be in writing. The reasons for making purchase contracts in writing were dealt with in Chapter 1 and the same considerations apply to amending them.

To avoid the problems which may be caused by an oral amendment it is commonplace to find in contracts a clause such as this:

> *This contract shall not be amended in any way other than by an agreement in writing which is expressly stated to amend this contract.*

In so far as these words concentrate the minds of the parties by making them consider whether there should be a contract amendment, they are helpful. They do not, however, override the ability of a representative of one party to agree to a binding agreement. An example:

> S is bound under its contract with P to deliver goods painted red. A representative of P orally agrees that S may deliver the goods painted green. Provided the representative of P appears to S to have the authority to commit P by way of oral amendment, then P is committed to the amendment. It is no

use P complaining afterwards that its representative was unaware why P needed the goods to be painted red. S need not be concerned with the politics within P's organisation.

There is no watertight way of preventing irresponsible colleagues causing mayhem in this way. One of the advantages of using a contract clause similar to the above is that if S, mindful of the contract terms, says to the representative of P: 'Well, if you're happy to let us supply the goods painted green, then perhaps you'd be good enough to sign this written amendment.' At this stage it is to be hoped that P's representative will have the sense to check with his colleagues.

A possible safeguard is to specify in the contract that no agent of P has authority to amend the contract with the exception of individuals named or identified by job title. However, it is doubtful whether even this is unassailable.

We come now to *novation*. This term is normally used to describe an agreement where A and B have a contract and one of the parties (B) wishes to *step out* of the contract and have its place taken by C. The result is that the contract is now between A and C and C now has the same rights and duties which, until then, had been the rights and duties of B.

The novation agreement is a carefully worded agreement between A, B and C which, among other provisions, needs to make clear whether C is liable for any breaches by B prior to the effective date of the novation.

It is not an amendment of the contract between A and B. It acts as a *discharge* of the agreement between A and B and the *substitution* of a new contract between A and C.

Without a tripartite agreement of this kind it is not possible for B to assign its *duties* under the contract although (see Chapter 14) B is usually free, without A's agreement, to assign its *rights* by means of section 136 of the Law of Property Act 1925.

CHAPTER 14

Assignment and subcontracting

The two words mean very different things.

Assignment

Originally it was not possible, as a general rule, for a contract party to transfer its rights or duties under a contract to a third party. This inability reflected the doctrine of privity of contract and the principle that each contract party must provide consideration to the other.

That was the position at common law. But, for a very long time, alongside the common law, there was a supplementary system known as *equity* which was applied by the High Court of Chancery. Equity *did* permit a party to assign its *rights* under a contract to an outsider but not its *duties*.

By 1873 common law and equity could be applied in the same court. Among many of the reforms at that time was the introduction of a statutory right of assignment of contract rights which are often referred to as *choses in action*. This statutory right is now to be found in section 136 of the Law of Property Act 1925. Section 136 permits the assignment of a right if:

- the assignment is absolute (an out and out transfer of the whole of the right);

- the assignment is in writing and signed by the assignor;

- express notice in writing has been given to the other contract party.

Usually, section 136 assignments arise where the assignor is the supplier who wishes to assign the outstanding contract price to a third party. The supplier is said to *sell* its invoices or *factor* its invoices. Inevitably, the price paid by the assignee (who is often called a *factor*) is less than the amount due to be paid to the assignor. The reason the assignment is made is to obtain faster payment and thereby improve cash flow.

There are three important points to remember:

1. If the debtor was entitled to pay the supplier a lesser sum than that stated in the contract, perhaps because of a breach of the contract by a supplier, then such a deduction may also be made against the assignee. *Any* defence that the debtor had as regards its liability to pay may be used against the assignee.

2. Notice in writing of the assignment must be received by the debtor.

3. Once notice in writing has been received, the debtor cannot discharge its contract liability by paying the original creditor (that is, the supplier). If it does so it remains liable to pay the assignee.

An exception to the ability to assign contract rights is where the identity of the party who wishes to assign the right is important to the party with the duty. This may be the position where the customer tries to assign its right to delivery of goods or to the performance of services; the assignment may be ineffective if the supplier is adversely affected by a change of customer. The following is an example:

> X is a fashionable interior decorator. He enters into a contract to carry out interior decoration at the home of Y, who is a film star. Before the contract is performed Y sells his house to Z who is a gangster. Y also assigns his rights under his contract with X to Z. If the assignment was allowed, X might legitimately claim that for him, the contract has become less attractive as he has lost the prestige value of being able to tell other customers that he has done work for Y. A further example will be found in the case of *Griffith* v *Tower Publishing Company* (see Appendix).

If the purchaser does not wish the supplier to assign, by far the safest way is to include a provision in the contract forbidding it. In most cases, however, the only right the supplier is capable of assigning is the right to payment, and whether the price is paid to him or to an assignee is usually a matter of indifference. Even with payment, however, some purchasers dislike dealing with factors who are often regarded as hard on late payees and difficult to deal with because of their remoteness.

In addition to the right of assignment given by the Law of Property Act, equitable assignment still exists. Unlike a section 136 assignment, an equitable assignment may still be effective even where, for example, it is only that of part of the contract debt or where no written notice has been given.

A section 136 assignment has a procedural advantage in that the assignee may sue in its own name; an equitable assignee has to make the assignor a party to the action.

Subcontracting

Subcontracting does not involve any assignment of contract rights or duties. Instead, the term describes one party performing its duties by using a third party who has no contractual relationship with the other party. It is sometimes referred to as *vicarious* performance.

With commercial contracts the starting point is that unless there is an express prohibition then the supplier is entitled to subcontract all or part of its contract duties. If the subcontractor does not supply the goods or services in accordance with the contract between the supplier and the purchaser then the latter will seek its remedy against the former. Although it may be possible for the purchaser to sue the subcontractor directly for the tort of negligence, the courts have shown considerable reluctance to allow a claim where the damages sought are for purely economic loss rather than for personal injury or damage to property.

It is quite common to see on purchasers' standard terms clauses prohibiting suppliers from subcontracting. In many cases this will simply be unrealistic as many suppliers do not have the resources to perform all the contract duties themselves.

If, however, there is a concern on the part of the customer as to the quality or identity of the subcontractors the supplier intends to use then the customer should have them identified in the contract. This may be done specifically by name, or more generally with a requirement that the subcontractors to be chosen shall be, for example, members of their relevant trade association.

Where it is important to prohibit subcontracting is in a contract where the identity of the supplier of the goods or services is of foremost importance to the customer. Here are two examples:

1. A is a famous singer. B (a theatrical company) engages her to perform. A then wishes to subcontract the performances to her younger sister who also is very talented, but nowhere near as big *a name* as A.

2. X enters into a contract to buy new furniture for the boardroom. X's choice of Y as the supplier is strongly influenced by the fact that Y's workshops are manned by superb craftsmen. X then discovers that the furniture was largely made by a subcontractor to Y and that Y had confined itself to french polishing it.

In Example 1, although it would be prudent to have a clause prohibiting subcontracting, a court would take the view that A's identity is so vital to the contract that both parties intended that A and only A could perform. It would almost certainly imply a term that A should not subcontract her duties.

Example 2 is more difficult. Probably, in the absence of an express clause requiring Y to make the furniture itself, X would have no remedy, provided of course the furniture conformed with its specification and was free of any defects.

Although not a matter of subcontracting, a purchaser needs to give careful consideration where the supplier is a small company which is to provide services. In choosing that supplier the purchaser may well have the expectation that the services will be performed by a certain individual from that company. If it is so important that the services are actually performed by that individual, and no other, then this needs to be expressed in the contract.

CHAPTER 15

Late delivery – no delivery

Time of delivery

Whether the contract is for goods or services (or for both) the supplier is under a strict liability to comply with the delivery date or the time allowed for performance stated in the contract. Where there is a contract for services and no time for performance is expressed, the supplier is obliged under section 14 of the Supply of Goods and Services Act 1982 to carry them out within a reasonable time.

The Sale of Goods Act 1979 is not quite as explicit – section 29(3) provides:

> Where under the contract of sale the seller is bound to send the goods to the buyer, but no time for sending them is fixed, the seller is bound to send them within a reasonable time.

This subsection, curiously, confines itself to contracts of sale where, expressly or by implication, it is for the seller to deliver to the buyer's premises. It does not address the common situation where the buyer *collects* the goods from the seller. There can, however, be no doubt that where there is no fixed date for delivery, and delivery is *ex works*, the seller is also obliged to make the goods available for delivery within a reasonable time.

There is an important distinction between an express contractual obligation to make delivery on or by a certain date and the implied obligation to make delivery in a reasonable time. Where there is an express delivery date the supplier must comply with it – any lateness is a breach. Where delivery must be made within a reasonable time, then even if delivery takes longer than anticipated, the supplier will not be in breach if the delay was caused by circumstances outside its control. Accordingly, what is reasonable is not to be judged at the time the contract is made but at the time when performance is completed – *Pantland Hick* v *Raymond & Reid* (see Appendix).

If the supplier of the goods or services is in breach either because it has failed to meet the express delivery date or has failed to deliver within a reasonable time, then the supplier is liable to pay damages for any loss suffered by the other party.

May the other party terminate the contract? The answer is that the innocent party may only treat the contract as repudiated if the time for delivery is *of the essence*. In other words, where the contractual duty to deliver on time is a *condition* rather than a *warranty*.

Although it is often said that in commercial contracts time of delivery is normally of the essence, this is not always the case. It is unsafe to assume that *any* breach of contract concerning the time of delivery entitles the purchaser to terminate the contract.

It has already been seen that section 14 of the Supply of Goods and Services Act 1982 implies '… a term …' that the services shall be carried out within a reasonable time. It could have been expressed as a condition or as a warranty. If it had been the former, the purchaser would have had the right to treat the contract as repudiated and if the latter there would not have been that right. By calling it a *term* makes it an *intermediate* or *innominate* term. An intermediate term is one where a breach may range from causing the purchaser very little damage to causing great damage. Only when the damage happens can an estimate be made whether the breach is sufficiently grave to allow the purchaser to bring the contract to an end. In most cases this means that the delay has got to be substantial before termination is permitted.

Section 29(3) of the Sale of Goods Act also avoids committing itself as to whether the obligation of a seller to send the goods to a buyer within a reasonable time is a condition or a warranty by saying the seller '… is bound …'.

As regards delivery generally, section 28 of the Sale of Goods Act merely says that a seller:

> … must be ready and willing to give possession of the goods to the buyer in exchange for the price …

Sometimes the subject matter of the contract allows a clear inference to be drawn that time of delivery is of the essence. Thus a contract for the sale of specific goods of a highly perishable nature will almost certainly be regarded as one where the time of delivery is of the essence.

The golden rule for purchasers who wish to have a right to end the contract for any *delay in delivery, however short, is to express this right in the contract.* It is normally sufficient to say:

> *Delivery shall be made not later than 3 August 2001 and the time of delivery is of the essence.*

A blunter alternative is:

> *If delivery is not made by 3 August 2001 then the purchaser may treat the contract as repudiated by the supplier.*

The use of the expression *treat the contract as repudiated* should be carefully noted. Strictly speaking whenever there is a breach of a condition which gives the innocent party the right to call off the deal, that right is a right to treat the breach as a repudiation of the contract by the other, entitling the other party to treat the contract as discharged. A purchaser of goods who decides to treat the breach as a repudiation by the supplier is discharged from his obligations to take delivery of the goods and to pay for them.

In this chapter and elsewhere the more widely used expression *terminate the contract* is generally used.

What if there is a desire to terminate for late delivery but it is not clear if time is of the essence? There is authority for saying that it is open to the customer to serve a notice on the supplier as follows:

(a) recording that the supplier has failed to meet the time for delivery specified in the contract (or has failed to make delivery within a reasonable time); and

(b) requiring that the goods be delivered or the services performed by a stated date ...

Such a notice will have the effect of making time of the essence, if it is not so already. If the other party fails to comply with the notice the contract may then be treated as terminated. Of course, the period of time given in (b) must be one which is achievable by the supplier – if not, it will be regarded as unreasonable.

What about instalment deliveries? As regards a contract subject to the Sale of Goods Act the matter is addressed in section 31. No similar guidance is given for goods supplied under contracts which are subject to the Supply of Goods and Services Act but it is safe to say the principles of section 31 of the former will also apply.

Section 31(1) provides:

Unless otherwise agreed, the buyer of goods is not bound to accept delivery of them by instalments.

Although it is useful to know that this right exists, many buyers will be quick to say that from a commercial viewpoint often delivery of *some* is better than delivery of *none*. If, however, the seller can only deliver part of an order, it might be worth pointing out this subsection and making it clear that accepting delivery of part of the order is upon the basis that no payment for it shall be due until the remainder has been delivered. When appropriate, it should also be made clear that acceptance of an instalment is not intended to waive any right of the purchaser to damages.

We must now consider section 31(2):

> Where there is a contract for the sale of goods to be delivered by stated instalments, which are to be separately paid for, and the seller makes defective deliveries in respect of one or more instalments ... it is a question in each case depending on the terms of the contract and the circumstances of the case whether the breach of contract is a repudiation of the whole contract or whether it is a severable breach giving rise to a claim for compensation but not to a right to treat the whole contract as repudiated.

Assuming that no guidance is to be found in the contract itself, it is necessary to understand what rights of termination there may be when there is a failure to deliver an instalment. These may be:

- to refuse to accept an instalment which is late, to reject instalments already made and to refuse delivery of any future instalments; or

- to refuse to accept the late instalment and any future instalments; or

- to refuse to accept only the late instalment.

From the supplier's point of view, these are in descending order of severity.

The main criteria which should be applied in establishing rights of termination are:

- the ratio between the number of instalments the supplier fails to deliver and the total number;

- the likelihood the supplier will fail to make future deliveries;

- the supplier's reason for the failure; and

- the reduction, if any, in the value to the purchaser of the instalments delivered and/or to be delivered in the future, caused by the failure of the supplier to deliver any one instalment.

Within the three possible remedies set out and the four criteria lie an infinite number of possibilities. Much will depend on the reason the supplier is late and on whether there is a likelihood that delivery of all the instalments will eventually be made. The use which the purchaser is able to make of the goods which have been delivered is critical. A lesser number may be of little or no value.

We have looked at delivery of goods by instalments. We now need to consider the position in contracts for services where the supplier has contracted to perform them on an irregular or a regular basis. It may be that the supplier has agreed to provide services on a *stand-by* basis so that he will, for example, provide emergency repairs when called upon. It might alternatively be that the supplier has agreed to attend regularly at the purchaser's premises to perform routine maintenance.

With contracts such as these, if there is a failure to attend on one or more than one occasion, similar tests should be applied in finding out if the purchaser has a right to terminate:

- how often has it happened?

- how likely is it to happen again?

- how potentially serious for the purchaser is the failure?

Excusable delay

At the beginning of this chapter it was noted that if delivery is late the supplier is in breach. Sometimes, however, the delay may be through no fault of the supplier. The delay may, for example, be due to the goods being accidentally damaged or destroyed shortly before delivery. In a contract for services, an example is an inability to perform the service on time because of exceptionally bad weather.

It has already been seen that where delivery or performance has to be made in a reasonable time then, in assessing what is reasonable, allowance will be made for events of the kind described above.

The problem comes with fixed delivery dates and fixed times for performance. Failure to meet these are breaches of contract and unless it can be said that the contract is *frustrated* (see below) then the supplier is liable whatever the reason. To mitigate the harshness of this, the parties often agree to a contract clause which is often called an *excusable delay clause*. Such a clause normally contains the following:

- a provision that the supplier shall have no liability for delay caused by circumstances beyond its reasonable control;

- a provision that the time for delivery or performance stated in the contract shall be extended by the same amount as the period of that delay; and

- a definition of what does, and does not, amount to excusable delay.

The last of these is not strictly necessary and excusable delay may simply be described as *circumstances beyond the supplier's reasonable control.* For the purchaser there are dangers in not having a proper definition. It leaves open the question whether the supplier can claim the failure of its own supplier or subcontractor as a circumstance beyond its reasonable control. If it can, this may be undesirable from the purchaser's point of view if it gives the supplier less incentive to establish its own supply network properly or to monitor the performance of it.

It is prudent to provide that the clause shall only give the supplier protection if he:

- gives the purchaser prompt and detailed notice of any event which has caused or might cause delay;

- provides an estimate of the likely period of delay; and

- is required to provide a recovery plan of the steps, if any, he proposes to take to minimise the delay.

Before agreeing to an excusable delay clause a question the purchaser should always ask is:

> *Could the effect of the clause be that we might have to sit back and wait a very long time until the supplier overcomes the event which is beyond his reasonable control?*

If the answer is *yes*, then it might be that such a clause, while absolving the supplier from liability to pay damages, should retain the purchaser's right to terminate for late delivery.

An agreement to provide relief to a supplier who would otherwise be in breach of contract for late delivery is a variety of what is often called a *force majeure clause*. This term describes any provision in a contract for a mechanism which allows for a variation to take account of a change in circumstances – whether it relates to late delivery, increased expenditure or any other unexpected change.

Frustration of contract

Sometimes, after a contract is made, something happens which makes the contract either *impossible* to perform or would result in performance being radically different from that which the parties contemplated at the time they entered the contract. In both cases the contract is regarded as *frustrated*, provided the frustrating event has not been brought about by the party who claims the contract is frustrated, as in the case of *Maritime National Fish* v *Ocean Trawlers* (see Appendix).

Because the effect of frustration is that usually delivery or performance becomes impossible or impossible in the foreseeable future it is convenient to consider it within this chapter.

A frustrating event which renders the contract *impossible* to perform is readily understandable and not uncommon. A simple example would be the withdrawal of an export licence required to enable delivery of goods.

Events which do not cause impossibility but result in performance of the contract being *radically different* from that which the parties contemplated are rare. One such case was *Krell* v *Henry* decided in 1903:

The defendant rented a flat in London for the purpose of charging people to come in and watch the coronation processions of the newly crowned King. The King was taken ill and his coronation postponed. The defendant refused to pay the rest of the price for the rooms. The court decided that the contract was frustrated. Both parties knew that the sole purpose of the defendant hiring the rooms was for the coronation.

Krell v *Henry* may be usefully compared with a case in the same year, *Herne Bay Steamboat Co* v *Hutton*:

Here again, the defendant had hoped to make money from the forthcoming coronation. He chartered a boat so he could sell tickets to sail on her. The trips were to have been around Spithead where the Royal Navy's ships were gathered for the purpose of a naval review by the King. The review was cancelled and the defendant claimed frustration of contract. Here, the court said there was not a frustrating event. The ship was still available for his use and that was a benefit he would still have had. Furthermore, the Royal Navy's ships were still moored at Spithead and that was another benefit.

In a more recent case, a contract for the purchase of a warehouse which the purchaser intended to redevelop was held not to be frustrated even though it was declared a *listed building* a day after the contract was signed. The effect of it being listed made it impossible for the purchaser to redevelop the building.

Merely because some supervening event has made the contract less attractive for one of the parties – or even downright unattractive – does not amount to frustration.

Where a contract is regarded as frustrated each party ceases to have any liability to the other unless, before the frustrating event occurred, one party had paid money to the other. This would be recoverable under the Law Reform (Frustrated Contracts) Act 1943, although the court has power to deduct from the sum to be returned expenses incurred by the payee in performance of the contract before the frustrating event. There is also power under the 1943 Act to order payment by a party who has received a *valuable benefit* under the contract prior to the frustrating event.

CHAPTER 16

Payment

It was seen in Chapter 7 that section 28 of the Sale of Goods Act 1979 provides that payment and delivery must be concurrent unless otherwise agreed. Accordingly, the supplier cannot demand some or all of the price in advance of delivery and the purchaser cannot demand credit.

In the absence of an express term entitling the supplier to an advance payment it is unlikely that a term would be implied giving the supplier that right.

Credit in the sense of a time gap between delivery and payment is another matter. The time within which the purchaser must pay after delivery of the goods or completion of the services will normally be expressed in a written contract and it is very unusual not to find such a term in either suppliers' or purchasers' standard terms of business.

Even if there is no express term as to credit, a court will be quick to imply such a term if the parties have had previous dealings and the supplier has accepted, without protest, a gap between delivery and payment. Section 28 is, arguably, showing its age – suppliers to companies, government departments and similar know perfectly well that when goods are delivered there will not be a representative of the purchaser waiting with a fistful of banknotes. Most purchasers expect a supplier to present an invoice on or after delivery, which will then be processed in the usual way. Commerce has moved on from sturdy merchants paying cash *on the nail* to a credit-based culture.

What of contracts other than those for the sale of goods? Unlike the Sale of Goods Act, the Supply of Goods and Services Act 1982 does not provide any guidance as to the time for payment in contracts for the transfer of goods, contracts of hire or contract for services. The common law rule is that the supplier is not entitled to an advance payment, nor is the purchaser entitled to credit, unless the contract expressly or impliedly provides otherwise. The ease with which a term as to credit will be implied into a contract for the sale of goods will also apply to those contracts.

What if the purchaser fails or refuses to pay?

Let us first consider the position where the supplier is entitled under the contract to an advance payment, that is a payment to be made prior to delivery of the goods or prior to completion of the services. Section 10(1) of the Sale of Goods Act provides:

Unless a different intention appears from the terms of the contract, stipulations as to time of payment are not of the essence of a contract of sale.

In many cases where a contract for the sale of goods has a term requiring an advance payment it is there because the supplier needs that money to assist procurement and to finance manufacture. If time is not of the essence the supplier is unable to terminate and is in the uncomfortable position of having to start procurement and manufacture to enable it to achieve the delivery date.

Similar comment may be made where an advance payment is due under contracts not governed by the Sale of Goods Act. It is, of course, always open to the unpaid supplier to sue for the money but there are usually strong commercial arguments for not doing so at such an early stage of a contractual relationship.

From the supplier's point of view the best answer lies in including in the contract words which allow:

- in contracts for the sale and the transfer of goods, that late payment shall cause the delivery date to be correspondingly later; and

- in contracts of hire and contracts for services, that the period of hire and the commencement of the services respectively shall not start unless and until that payment is made.

Let us now consider the normal position where payment is due on or after delivery of the goods or completion of the services. The following assumes that either the purchaser is not entitled to credit or that the contractual credit period has expired.

In the case of goods, it is safe to assume that once delivery has taken place title in them will have vested in the purchaser unless there is a reservation of title clause which will be considered later. What the supplier *cannot* do is seize back the goods without the purchaser's consent. Such conduct would be a tort and actionable by the purchaser.

In the case of a completed contract of hire or a completed contract for services, once these have been performed they cannot be undone and so any considerations of seizing back are inappropriate.

An unpaid supplier may be able to exercise a *lien* where:

- there has been a contract for the sale or other transfer of those goods but the supplier is still in possession of them; or

- there has been a contract for the performance of services on the purchaser's goods and the supplier is still in possession of those goods.

A lien is a right of possession entitling an unpaid supplier of goods, who is lawfully in possession of them, to retain them and, in certain circumstances, to sell them. The supplier may lawfully be in possession of them for a number of reasons. It may, for example, be storing the goods for the purchaser. A supplier under a contract for services who has possession of a purchaser's goods for the purpose of repair, modification or similar also has a lien for the contract price and again, in certain circumstances, a right of sale.

The Sale of Goods Act 1979 deals fairly comprehensively with suppliers' liens and powers of sale in sections 38 to 48.

One of the greatest risks an unpaid supplier faces is the purchaser becoming insolvent and going into liquidation. When this happens the best the unpaid supplier can hope for is a dividend on the price. This payment is calculated by liquidating (usually selling) such assets as the purchaser possesses and, from the total sum realised, paying to the supplier the same percentage of the price as the percentage the liquidated assets bore to the purchaser's total liability. Among the assets which will be liquidated are the goods the supplier sold to the purchaser if the title in those goods has vested in the purchaser.

If the contract has provided that title to the goods shall remain with the supplier until the goods are paid for, this is a reservation of title clause, often referred to as a *Romalpa clause*. Its effect, if properly drafted, is to allow the supplier to resist a sale of goods by the liquidator on the basis that as title to the goods is still vested in the supplier the goods do not form part of the purchaser's assets.

For obvious reasons suppliers are very keen on these clauses although a lot of them seem quite content with this short form:

> *Title to the goods shall remain vested in the supplier until the full purchase price has been paid.*

They rarely require the clause to specify the length of time before the supplier can demand return of the goods, the rights the supplier has to enter the purchaser's premises to retrieve the goods and matters of this nature.

Many purchasers are willing to agree to a Romalpa clause of the kind indicated. Their reasoning is that the supplier will get paid and so the clause doesn't do any harm. This may be the case but nevertheless such a clause is nonsense in many cases including the following:

- the goods are to be processed so as to change their form or appearance – pig iron, which is to be cast or forged to a shape;

- the goods are to be mixed with other goods in such a way that they can never be separated – a chemical added to paint;

- the goods become affixed to a building;

- the goods are bought to be resold to a third party as soon as possible.

In the first two instances, the supplier will lose its title as soon as the goods in question cease to be identifiable in their original form, due to the processing or mixing. In the third instance, affixing the goods so that they become part of a building also results in the supplier losing title.

The hazards of Romalpa clauses indicated above are mostly hazards for the supplier rather than the purchaser but in the fourth instance, the purchaser who buys goods to sell on as quickly as possible, there is something inherently unsatisfactory in selling goods without having the title in them. This is despite section 25 of the Sale of Goods Act which, in these circumstances, gives good title to a third party provided the third party has no knowledge of such defect in title.

If the supplier insists on a Romalpa clause but does not raise the separate issue of risk of accidental loss or damage to the goods, it is necessary to consider the effect of section 20 of the Sale of Goods

Act. This is the section which provides that unless the parties agree otherwise, the goods are at the supplier's risk until title passes (see Chapter 7). If the supplier retains title until the goods are paid for, then it is arguable that it continues to bear the risk.

Method of payment

The common law position is that payment shall be made in cash and, indeed, in cash of the right amount – the supplier is not obliged to provide change. In modern commercial contracts a term is very easily implied that payment by cheque is permissible.

Payments are often made by the debtor's bank to the creditor's and again there will usually be an implied term that payment from bank to bank is acceptable. However, payment is only deemed to have been made when the creditor has that payment credited to its account – that is, when the creditor's bank has processed the transaction.

It is harder to imply a term into a contract that the debtor is entitled to make payment by credit card or charge card although the conspicuous display of card logos used by card companies at the supplier's premises and on their brochures may well imply a term that payment may be made in such a way.

In 1988 the Court of Appeal held that a purchaser who pays by a credit card or charge card has discharged its obligation to make payment. There is no liability to make payment again if, for example, the card company becomes insolvent.

Interest on late payments

The common law position is that interest is not payable in the absence of an express provision in the contract. A major change has been made by the Late Payment of Commercial Debts (Interest) Act 1998. This legislation, which provides for the payment of interest, attempts to redress what has been described as *a national culture of bad payment* and to help small businesses which are widely perceived as being at the mercy of large organisations.

It came into force (partly) on 1 November 1998 and more time is needed before its effect on late payment may be assessed. Reactions to the legislation are mixed: some purchasers have taken the view that it is a useful discipline and they recognise its value in dealing with their own customers. More ominously, other purchasers have said of their suppliers: 'If they want any future business from us they'd better not try it!'

Section 1(1) provides:

> It is an implied term in a contract to which this Act applies that any qualifying debt created by the contract carries simple interest ...

The Act applies to a contract for the sale or transfer of goods, a hire contract or a contract for services.

Interest starts to run:

> ... on the day after the relevant day for the debt ...
>
> (section 4(2))

With the exception of advance payments (see later) *the relevant day* is the date which the supplier and purchaser have agreed is the date for payment (section 4(3)).

If the parties have not agreed the payment date then section 4(5) provides:

> ... the relevant day is the last day of the period of 30 days beginning with –
>
> (a) the day on which the obligation of the supplier to which the debt relates is performed; or
>
> (b) the day on which the purchaser has notice of the amount of the debt or (where that amount is unascertained) the sum which the supplier claims is the amount of the debt, whichever is the later.

The last four words of subsection (5) *whichever is the later* are crucial. Their inclusion means that where the purchaser has notice of the amount of the debt, because the price was expressed in the contract, the 30-day period starts to run from the day of delivery of the goods not from some later time when the supplier presents an invoice. This seems to preserve the common law position that the supplier is not under an *implied* duty to issue an invoice. A duty to invoice only arises where the contract provides so. Here are some examples:

- the contract provides that payment is due by 30 June – that is the relevant day and interest runs from 1 July (section 4(3));

- the contract is silent on the date of payment and the supplier delivers on 1 June – the relevant day is 30 June and interest runs from 1 July (section 4(5)(a));

- the contract is for the sale of goods in bulk at £3 per kilo and they have to be weighed to ascertain the price – the 30 days runs from the day the purchaser is notified of the price or the date of delivery, whichever is the later.

Whether or not the contract specifies the time within which payment must be made, it is always good purchasing practice to express in the contract that the duty to pay is subject to prior receipt of a correct invoice.

Interest can be obtained on late payment of an *advance payment*. Section 11(2) defines such a payment as:

> ... a payment falling due before the obligation of the supplier to which the whole contract price relates ('the supplier's obligation') is performed ...

Section 11 provides (with one exception 11(5)) that where the parties have agreed that the supplier shall be paid all or part of the contract price before the supplier has completed the contract and the purchaser fails to make that advanced payment, then it only attracts interest *when the supplier has completely performed.* In the case of a contract for goods this will usually be delivery and in the case of services completion of performance. In the case of a contract of hire the supplier's obligation is performed on the last day of the period of hire.

Section 11(5) deals with advance payments due in respect of part performance:

Where the advance payment is a part of the contract price due in respect of any part performance of the supplier's obligation, but is payable before that part performance is completed, the debt shall be treated as created on the day on which the relevant part performance is completed.

Part II of the Act deals with the extent to which the parties to the contract may exclude the provisions of the Act. Under section 8(1) any contract terms are void to the extent they purport to exclude the right to statutory interest under the Act:

... unless there is a substantial contractual remedy for late payment of the debt.

The meaning of *substantial remedy* is set out in section 9:

(1) A remedy for the late payment of the debt shall be regarded as a substantial remedy unless –
   (a) the remedy is insufficient either for the purpose of compensating the supplier for late payment or for deterring late payment; and
   (b) it would not be fair or reasonable to allow the remedy to be relied on to oust or (as the case may be) to vary the right to statutory interest that would otherwise apply in relation to the debt.
(2) In determining whether a remedy is not a substantial remedy, regard shall be had to all the relevant circumstances at the time the terms in question are agreed.

Subsection (1)(a) introduces the notion of a deterrent and this is a bold departure in the law of contract. A cornerstone of the law relating to the rights and remedies for any breach of contract is that punishment of the party in breach is inappropriate – damages are only available as compensation for loss.

In determining whether the parties have agreed *a substantial remedy* to supplant the right to statutory interest it must pass the requirement of being fair and reasonable. Section 9(3) sets out a non-exhaustive list of matters which must be taken into account:

(a) the benefits of commercial certainty;
(b) the strength of the bargaining positions of the parties relative to each other;
(c) whether the term was imposed by one party to the detriment of the other (whether by the use of standard terms or otherwise); and
(d) whether the supplier received an inducement to agree to the term.

As will be seen below, the statutory rate of interest is 8 per cent above the Bank of England official dealing rate. If a supplier is happy to agree in the contract to a lower rate of interest, to the exclusion of the statutory interest rate, this may be perfectly adequate compensation but it might not meet the deterrent requirement.

Section 14 anticipates that a purchaser with significant muscle may try to defeat the intention of the Act by insisting on the inclusion in the contract of a very long credit period. Such a term is made subject to the requirement of reasonableness under section 3(2)(b) of the Unfair Contract Terms Act 1977 *even* if the offending term is not contained in the purchaser's standard terms of business.

The Act does not come into immediate effect, but in stages:

- From 1 November 1998 interest may be claimed by small businesses against large businesses and against public authorities in respect of contracts made on or after that date.

- From 1 November 2000 small businesses may also claim interest against other small businesses in respect of contracts made on or after that date.

- From 1 November 2002 all businesses and public authorities may claim interest against all businesses and public authorities in respect of contracts made on or after that date.

This phased introduction is by means of statutory instruments.

The definition of a *small business* is one with 50 or less full-time employees and a large business is one with 50 employees or more. SI 1998 No. 2479 provides detailed rules as to how the headcount of employees must be done.

In respect of contracts made between 1 November 1998 and 31 October 2000, where there is a claim for interest against a business, the onus of proof is on the debtor to show that it is not a large business (SI 1998 No. 2481). A business wishing to discharge this onus to avoid paying interest may well be deterred when it sees the complexity of the rules referred to in SI 1998 No. 2479!

The rate of interest has been set by SI 1998 No. 2765. It is 8 per cent over the Bank of England Official Dealing Rate. This rate is published daily in *The Financial Times* together with the date on which the rate was last set. It will be found in the section entitled 'London Money Rates' and is referred to as the 'UK Clearing Bank Base Lending Rate'.

CHAPTER 17

Remedies for breach of contract

No more will be said in this chapter about a purchaser's remedy of rejecting goods and treating the contract as repudiated by reason of a supplier's breach. This has been dealt with in Chapters 7, 15 and elsewhere. However, more needs to be said about the other remedies.

Damages

If there is a breach of contract and the innocent party has suffered loss due to that breach it is entitled to damages. If no loss has been suffered then, at best, the damages will be nominal.

Often it is easy to quantify the loss but sometimes it is not. Difficulty in translating a loss into a money figure will not stop a court from making an award. Thus, claims for damages for loss of goodwill and loss of future profit may be sustained.

The fundamental object of damages is to compensate the innocent party by putting it in the position it would have been in had the breach not occurred. Here are some examples:

- A agrees to buy a car from B. A later says he will refuse to accept delivery. The evidence is that B is able to obtain as many cars as he can find buyers. Although B is able to sell the car to C, B is able to claim damages from A for loss of profit. Had A honoured the contract B would have been able to sell another car to C and so would have gained two profits rather than one. Of course, if title to a particular car had passed to A then B could have sued for the price – see the section on transfer of title and risk in Chapter 7.

- D refuses to take delivery of a car he has agreed to buy from E. Here the evidence is that these particular cars are in very short supply – would-be customers are queuing up for them. E sells the car to F. E is not able to claim damages for loss of profit against D. If D had accepted delivery, E would not have been able to sell the car to F. E has not lost the sale.

For damages for breach of contract to be recoverable they must not be too *remote*. The principles relating to remoteness of damage are often referred to as *the rule in Hadley* v *Baxendale*. In that case the plaintiff, a miller, contracted with the defendant for the latter to transport a broken crankshaft from the plaintiff's mill to a crankshaft maker who needed it as a pattern to make a new one. The defendant was unaware that the mill could not operate until the plaintiff had the new crankshaft. The defendant delayed in performing the contract of carriage and the plaintiff sued for loss of profit during the period of delay. The court decided that damages were only recoverable:

1. where they are such as may be fairly and reasonably considered as arising naturally from the breach; or

2. where they may reasonably be supposed to be within the parties' contemplation at the time of the contract.

This means:

- The loss suffered by the innocent party must be of a kind which the defendant should have realised might be suffered through a breach (Rule 1). *Or*

- The defendant knew at the time the contract was made that the loss was of a kind which might result if there was a delay in delivery to the crankshaft maker (Rule 2).

The court said that just because the crankshaft was broken did not impute to the defendant knowledge that the mill would stand idle – other parts of the machinery might also have been broken or the plaintiff might have had a spare shaft. The plaintiff could only have succeeded under Rule 2 if he had informed the defendant of the true position at the time the contract was made.

Although decided as long ago as 1854, the rule in *Hadley* v *Baxendale* remains the basis of the law relating to remoteness of damage in the law of contract.

If the loss is of a kind which is covered by Rule 1 or Rule 2 then the defendant is liable even though the financial loss is higher than the parties might have expected at the time the contract was made.

There is no relationship between the contract price and the amount of damages for breach of contract.

In many cases a supplier providing goods or services to a commercial purchaser will be aware that failure to deliver or perform may result in a loss of profit for the purchaser. For example, machinery will usually be bought either for the purchaser to use for manufacturing purposes or to resell. In either case it is reasonably foreseeable at the time the contract is made that a failure to deliver will result in a loss of profit.

If a purchaser anticipates that a breach by a supplier may result in a loss which does not come within Rule 1 because it is not obvious, then Rule 2 may be used by making the supplier aware of it before the contract is made or by setting it out in the contract. An example may be found in *Simpson* v *The London and North Western Railway Company* (see Appendix).

Similarly, if the goods delivered are defective, then it may be foreseeable that the purchaser will suffer a loss of profit either through an inability to use the machine itself or, in the case of a resale, the loss of that resale.

The right to damages is, to some extent, conditioned by the requirement that the claimant must behave reasonably – the claimant must *mitigate* its damage. Consider the following:

> A, a taxi company, agrees to buy a new taxi from B. B fails to deliver it. Each taxi operated by A makes a daily profit of £75 and A currently operates six taxis.

A cannot continue to operate only the existing six vehicles and claim damages for a continuing loss of profit it would have made each day if it had had the seventh. It has a duty to buy one elsewhere as soon as is reasonably practicable. If it can only buy one from someone else, for a higher price, it can recover that excess from B. A can also recover the £75 a day loss of profit during a reasonable time taken to procure the alternative vehicle.

But the requirement that A should act reasonably does not go too far:

> A agrees to buy a taxi from B and the contract specifies the vehicle is to be painted red. The vehicle delivered is blue. A rejects it for breach of the condition implied by section 13 of the Sale of Goods Act 1979 because it does not correspond with its contract description.

A is entitled to the same damages as it was under the previous example. B cannot say that A is obliged to mitigate the loss by accepting the blue vehicle because A's customers would not have refused to ride in it because of its colour. A has the right to reject the blue taxi and refuse any offer made by B to paint it red or to procure another one painted red.

Liquidated damages

Liquidated damages are those quantified sums of money which are expressed in a contract to be payable by one party to another upon the happening of a certain event. Nearly always they are used to quantify the compensation payable by the supplier to the customer if there is a delay in delivering the goods or providing the services contracted for.

Where there is a liquidated damages clause it will generally be construed as the full extent of the financial compensation the purchaser may obtain from the supplier even though the purchaser's actual loss is greater or lesser. It is also a matter of construction whether such a clause restricts or removes any right the purchaser would otherwise have to terminate for lateness. Accordingly, a purchaser who wishes to retain a right to terminate for lateness should seek to include in the contract a provision entitling it to terminate for lateness notwithstanding its right to liquidated damages.

For a liquidated damages clause to be enforceable it must be shown to be a genuine pre-estimate of the likely amount of loss which may be suffered by the purchaser. If the liquidated damages are extravagant and intended to act as a deterrent rather than compensatory, then they are deemed to be a penalty and not enforceable.

The time at which the genuine pre-estimate is to be made is the time of the contract. Despite the conventional wisdom it is quite forgivable to question whether, in most contracts, it is even possible to make a realistic estimate at such an early stage. Usually this problem has been avoided by the relevant clause providing that amounts payable should be moderate so that they are unlikely to be regarded as a sword hanging over the supplier's head.

If a liquidated damages clause is enforceable then the party is entitled to them even if it has not actually suffered any loss. Where such a clause is used for dealing with late delivery it is common to provide that the contract price shall be reduced by a certain percentage for each week or month of such a delay. It is also usual to provide that the purchaser shall be entitled to deduct the amounts due from the purchase price.

When drafting a liquidated damages clause it is important to remember that if the liquidated damages are really punitive, the clause will be unenforceable even if they are described as a pre-estimate of likely loss. Conversely, to describe the amount payable as a *penalty* is not necessarily fatal if the court takes the view that it *is* a genuine pre-estimate.

Specific performance

Specific performance and injunctions, unlike damages, are not remedies the innocent party is entitled to as of right. They are at the discretion of the court.

An order for specific performance may be granted where, for example, A and B have a contract in which A has agreed to sell unique goods to B and A subsequently refuses to deliver the goods (for example an oil painting) to B. Here, the court might be prepared to order A to make delivery. A breach of such an order would be a contempt of court exposing A, or even its responsible employees, to criminal penalties.

Because specific performance is discretionary the court will only make an order if it is possible for it to be enforced. If the reason A has not delivered the painting to B is because A has sold it to C, then an order will not be made.

A few years ago the House of Lords had an opportunity of examining orders for specific performance in a case called *Co-op Insurance Society Ltd* v *Argyll Stores (Holdings) Ltd.*

The Co-op was the lessor of a shopping centre and it had let the largest unit in the development to Argyll for use as a supermarket. At the time the lease was made the Co-op was aware that the success of the shopping centre depended on there being a supermarket because it would attract more people to the whole development. Accordingly, the 35-year lease contained a provision that Argyll would use the premises for that purpose. After about 18 years Argyll closed down its supermarket. The Court of Appeal made an order of specific performance against Argyll compelling it to reopen it.

This order was quashed in the House of Lords. The various judgments made clear that just because an order for specific performance is discretionary does not mean courts may order it willy-nilly. An order in this case was not regarded as practicable as it would require too much supervision by the court.

Injunctions

An injunction is similar to specific performance – it is an order of the court that something be done or that something should not be done. It is an appropriate remedy to grant if B has agreed to sell a painting to A and, before delivery, A becomes aware that B is planning to sell it to C.

An injunction is also a useful tool to prevent one party divulging the other's confidential information.

An advantage of an injunction is that if urgency requires it a court may grant one on an interim basis before the full trial of the action.

CHAPTER 18

Electronic commerce

The object of this chapter is not to provide a detailed guide to the methods of electronic commerce – developments in e-commerce are so rapid that, if it was tried, the information would probably be out of date by the time of publication! Rather, the purpose is to highlight the legal difficulties posed by e-commerce while, at the same time, demonstrating that it does not involve tearing up the whole law of contract and starting again.

A headline to a recent article in an information technology magazine declared:

> E-commerce has made cross-border trading more accessible, but has also presented legal problems never encountered before ...

Statements like this are often made but they are far from justified.

E-commerce has been defined as *doing business electronically* and so, by this definition, it has been around for a very long time. Alexander Graham Bell obtained a patent for the telephone in 1876 and by then the telegraph was already well established. Each medium, from its inception, became an avenue for effecting legally binding contracts. The same is also true of telex and fax media.

The misconception appears to be based on the fact that goods and services may be procured without, on the supplier's side, any human intervention and, indeed, with systems such as *electronic data interchange* ('EDI') a purchase may be made without human intervention on either side.

The absence of human intervention does not, in any way, affect the basic position concerning those essential factors needed for the formation of a valid contract: *offer* and *acceptance*. All the parties have done is to delegate their decision-making to agents – albeit electronic ones.

Suppliers have, for many years, made sales automatically by means of automatic vending machines. Machines which dispense a cup of coffee, a bar of chocolate or whatever are the way the operator of a machine makes an offer to sell. The acceptance of the offer is made by the buyer doing that which the machine makes clear he should do: putting money in the machine and, where appropriate, pressing the right button to choose which particular item he wants.

Normally, the display of goods for the purpose of sale is not an offer to sell. It is regarded as *an invitation to treat* – it is the buyer who makes the offer which the seller is free to accept or reject. But, with an automatic vending machine, the seller has organised himself so that he does not have the ability to refuse to sell and accordingly the only sensible analysis is that the seller makes the offer by making the machine available for sales. The machine, on its owner's behalf, is making a standing offer to sell to anyone who chooses to accept that offer.

Where purchases are made by electronic mail the offer and the acceptance will be found in the same way as they are found in an oral contract or in one made by an exchange of correspondence.

The problem with electronic mail contracts is *when* acceptance takes place. The basic rule is that acceptance, to be effective, must be *communicated* to the offeror. If it is not there is no contract.

The requirement that acceptance must be communicated is subject to a well-known exception – *the postal rule*. Where acceptance is made by posting a letter, acceptance is deemed complete *at the time of posting*. There is a valid contract even though the letter of acceptance is late arriving *or even if it never arrives*.

There is a generally held view that the postal rule does not apply to electronic methods of communication and *Entores* v *Miles Far East Corporation* is usually relied upon in support of this. That case, however, was concerned not with *when* acceptance was made but *where*. For procedural reasons it was necessary for the Court of Appeal to decide whether a contract made by an exchange of telex messages was concluded in Amsterdam (from where the acceptance was sent) or London (where the acceptance was received). The court took the view that, as the medium of telex was almost instantaneous, the formation of the contract was similar to a contract made in a telephone conversation: acceptance must be communicated to be effective – the contract was made in London.

However, this case does not really help resolve the difficulty of acceptance made by e-mail where the acceptance has been sent to the other party but is not accessed by that party until later. Is acceptance complete when the offeror *could* have accessed it or when he *does*? The distinction could be crucial. This subject is addressed in the European Electronic Commerce Directive (see below).

When purchases are made on the web it is not clear which party is the offeror and which is the offeree. One approach is the vending machine one: the seller, by describing the goods, is making an offer to sell which the purchaser accepts by pressing an icon confirming his decision to buy. An alternative approach is that the purchaser is making the offer to buy by indicating, electronically, the goods he wants. Acceptance is by the seller, after it satisfies itself as to the purchaser's payment card details. Put another way: the seller's website is his shop window. It will be seen below that the Electronic Commerce Directive does not resolve this issue.

After the parties have carried out a transaction on the web it is common for the seller to confirm the order by e-mail. Depending on how this is done it is likely to be no more than evidence or confirmation of an already completed contract. If it is worded in the language of acceptance then it is possible (subject to close scrutiny of what earlier took place on the web) that the e-mail is the contractual acceptance.

When purchasing on the web it is quite likely the contract will be on the supplier's terms if these are displayed on the supplier's website. It is important not only to read them, but to have a copy available if there is a subsequent dispute.

The terms can, of course, be downloaded onto the computer, together with details of the order, the price and the place of delivery. An alternative is to make a hard copy and file it. The hard copy will automatically bear the date on which it was made which will be useful evidence if the supplier later changes those terms of sale. Some readers will no doubt regard the making of a hard copy as an erosion of the advantages of e-commerce, but it does seem a neat and convenient way of recording the terms of the transaction.

Where a purchaser intends to buy regularly from a supplier the best course is for them to have a framework agreement which sets out the terms governing any electronic transactions they might make in the future. This has been the usual practice of EDI users.

Other legal problems of e-commerce are:

- security;

- taxation;

- governing law.

Security of a document is achieved by *cryptography* which encodes it so that it is unintelligible to an unauthorised reader. Cryptography is also the science used to provide a unique *signature*, thereby enabling the authenticity of the sender to be established. It takes the place of a manual signature on a hard document.

Governments throughout the world are concerned that *encryption* is a useful tool for unlawful activities and are anxious to have access to the logic necessary to decipher encoded documents. In the United Kingdom the Regulation of Investigatory Powers Act 2000 (see below) has been enacted to meet this concern. There is considerable resistance to the idea of governmental powers of surveillance, not least on the ground that it is an interference with civil liberties.

Cryptography services are often provided by third parties and the integrity and security of these is paramount.

The second area of difficulty appears to be tax collection on profits from electronic commerce. Life could become more difficult for government tax agencies as e-commerce means that the supplier's place of business is in cyberspace rather than on physical premises which can be visited and searched. Where the item purchased does not require physical delivery, such as written text which may be downloaded electronically, a tax evader could certainly give the authorities a run for their money. This, coupled with electronic payment, encryption and the ease of trading on a global scale may well cause a lack of control by governments. We only need to compare the almost uncontrollable proliferation of pornography on the web.

Identifying the law which governs an electronic contract is often said to be a problem. Clearly if there is an express choice of law there is no problem. If there is no express choice then there may be a difficulty. But then so there may be with any cross-border transaction – whatever medium is used.

Some of the above issues have been addressed in the United Kingdom by the Electronic Communications Act 2000.

Part I (which is to be brought into force by statutory instrument) establishes a register of third-party cryptography service providers and establishes a framework for regulation of them. It also makes provision for the degree of security third-party service providers must use. The register is voluntary and a third-party provider who chooses not to register is still free to provide cryptography services.

Section 7 provides for electronic signatures and related certificates to be admissible in legal proceedings. It effectively implements the European Union Electronic Signatures Directive (1999/93/EC). Section 7 is also to be brought into force by statutory instrument.

Section 8 gives the appropriate Minister the power to amend legislation to allow electronic alternatives where such legislation currently requires paper or a signature. A suitable subject for such an amendment is section 136 of the Law of Property Act 1925 which requires an assignment of a chose in action to be:

> ... by writing under the hand of the assignor ... and
> ... where express notice in writing has been given to the debtor.

Section 8 does not permit changes in legislation which would *force* a move to paperless systems – changes are only to be made to provide an electronic alternative.

It should also be noted that the power to change legislation does not apply to matters controlled by the Inland Revenue or Customs & Excise who already have the ability to permit electronic options under sections 132 and 133 of the Finance Act 1999.

Generally, the Electronics Communications Act 2000 is fairly mild and is seen by the government as legislation to facilitate the use of e-commerce rather than to regulate it. The government, in a Consultation Document dated 5 March 1999, expressed its commitment to e-commerce as follows:

... of developing the UK as the world's best place in which to trade electronically and the Prime Minister has set the target that by 2002, 25% of dealings by citizens and businesses with government should be able to be done electronically.

There may turn out to be a big difference between 25 per cent of such dealings *actually* being done electronically and the Prime Minister's target of a *capability* to do 25 per cent of dealings electronically. Time will tell.

Further UK legislation has arrived: the Regulation of Investigatory Powers Act 2000, which is an attempt to deal with the deep concern of the government that the increasing use of electronic media, and of encryption techniques in particular, will be of great value to criminals.

The Act's provisions give to law enforcement agencies rights to intercept e-mails and Internet messages. There are also powers to require senders or receivers of coded messages to provide the code to such agencies to enable decoding. The 'big brother' aspect of this legislation has caused much adverse comment. It has also been suggested that service providers may be discouraged from basing themselves in the UK and may move elsewhere. Again, time will tell.

Further legislation in the field of e-commerce is most likely to be the result of international agreement. E-commerce is global and there is little point in any one country making its own rules.

The European Electronic Commerce Directive (2000/31 EC) of 8 June 2000 must be incorporated into UK legislation by January 2002. This is also primarily intended to facilitate electronic commerce rather than to regulate it. The Electronic Communications Act is generally consistent with the Directive.

Article 10 of the Directive requires Member States to ensure, except where otherwise agreed by the parties who are not consumers, that in the case of e-commerce, certain information is made available to prospective purchasers, including the different technical steps which will result in contract formation. Article 10 also requires that contract terms and general terms must be made available to a purchaser in a way that allows them to be stored and reproduced.

Article 11 is of particular importance:

1. Member States shall ensure, except when otherwise agreed by parties who are not consumers, that in cases where the recipient of the service places his order through technological means, the following principles apply:
   - the service provider has to acknowledge the receipt of the recipient's order without undue delay and by electronic means,
   - the order and the acknowledgement of receipt are deemed to be received when the parties to whom they are addressed are able to access them.

2. Member States shall ensure that, except when otherwise agreed by the parties who are not consumers, the service provider makes available to the recipient of the service appropriate, effective and accessible means allowing him to identify and correct input errors, prior to the placing of the order.

3. Paragraph 1, first indent, and paragraph 2 shall not apply to contracts concluded exclusively by exchange of electronic mail or by equivalent individual communications.

In the context of Article 11, the *recipient* is the purchaser and *the service provider* is the supplier or the agent of the supplier.

Paragraph 1, first indent, requires the supplier to acknowledge receipt of the purchaser's order but no attempt is made to provide which document contains the offer and which the acceptance.

Paragraph 1, second indent, when incorporated into national legislation, will provide some answer to a question posed earlier: in so far as an acceptance is made by electronic mail it shall be deemed to have been received when the addressee is *able* to receive it. This part of Article 11 will probably require amplification – guidance is needed as to the position if the addressee is ill, on holiday or for any other reason is unable to log on.

Paragraph 2 requires there to be a straightforward mechanism, where purchases are made by means of the web, for the purchaser to retract any errors made before placing an order.

In the case of contracts, where neither party is a consumer, the parties are able to agree terms as to contract formation which differ from paragraphs 1 and 2.

The Directive requires more legislation by Member States and this, coupled with advances in technology, should keep Parliament busy for the foreseeable future.

CHAPTER 19

Purchasing abroad

This chapter will comment on special factors relating to procuring goods and services from an overseas supplier.

Choice of law

Contract law is territorial. Each country has its own law and while the contract laws of most developed nations are more similar than dissimilar, nevertheless differences do exist. If ever there is litigation or a threat of it, it is important to be clear which law governs the contract. By far the safest course is for the contract to have an express choice of law clause.

For the purchaser in England, Wales or Northern Ireland it is preferable to choose English law. Strictly speaking, Northern Ireland has its own law of contract but its differences from English law are very slight.

The advantages of opting for English law include familiarity and the ease of obtaining legal advice.

Sometimes, however, it may not be possible to persuade the supplier to agree and the purchaser may be forced down the road of accepting a foreign law. In these circumstances it is important to obtain advice from a qualified source. This need not mean obtaining advice in the supplier's country – London is usually able to provide legal experts on most of the world's systems.

It is also open to the parties to agree to a governing law which is that of a third country – even one which has no connection with either of them or with the contract.

What if the parties do not make an express choice of law? If there is litigation it will be for the court to decide which law governs the contract. This will be done in accordance with the Contracts (Applicable Law) Act 1990 which brought into force in the United Kingdom the Rome Convention of 1980.

The 1990 Act provides that in the absence of an express choice of law by the parties, the governing law shall be that of the country having the closest connection with the contract. The Act introduces a presumption that this is the law of the country of that party making what is called the *characteristic performance*. This means that in a contract for the supply of goods, it is likely to be the law of the seller. In a contract for services it is likely to be the place of performance of those services.

When it is not possible to establish a country of characteristic performance the applicable law will be the law of the country which has the closest connection with the contract.

Sometimes, a dispute may arise whether the contract is formally valid. Did it need to be in writing to be enforceable? Did it need to be notarised? The Act provides that the requirement of formal validity is satisfied if the contract is valid either under the law applicable to the contract (whether through the express choice of the parties or because of the Act) or it is formally valid under the law of the place where it was made.

Choice of jurisdiction

As well as making an express choice of law the parties are also free to decide that any litigation must take place in the courts of a particular country. They could also agree that a party must start proceedings in, for example, the courts of either of the parties.

When nationalism or other considerations apply it is open to them to agree to confine jurisdiction to the courts of a third country.

An alternative to opting for the normal courts is to include an arbitration clause in the contract. This clause may include such matters as the place of arbitration, the language in which it will be conducted and the method of choosing the arbitrator or arbitrators. If the method of arbitration is not specified (for example in accordance with the rules of the International Chamber of Commerce) it will be decided by the law of the contract. The relevant statute in the United Kingdom is the Arbitration Act 1996.

If a party obtains a judgment of a court or an arbitral award it then has the task of enforcing it. In most cases this means getting the losing party to pay up. There is considerable scope, throughout the developed world, to enforce a judgment or award made in one country in another country where the losing party has assets which may be used to satisfy that judgment.

In certain circumstances it is possible to obtain a freezing injunction preventing a party removing assets from the jurisdiction where the removal would defeat or hinder the enforcement of a judgment that the other has obtained or might obtain.

Delivery

Natural, political and taxation frontiers between nations mean that purchasing abroad requires serious consideration of delivery terms. Who pays the sales tax and duties? Who insures the goods? Who generates any shipping documents which may be required? Who insures the goods during their transit?

Incoterms are a great help. Incoterms are 13 delivery terms drawn up by the International Chamber of Commerce. They provide a definition of each of the terms together with a clear and concise statement of the respective rights and duties of each party for each of the terms. The current edition is *Incoterms 2000* and is to be found in Publication 560 of the ICC.

The terms range from the one least onerous for the seller, *ex works*, to the most onerous for the seller, *delivered duty paid*. Expression of them in a contract is simplicity itself. If the parties have, for example, agreed that the seller should bring the goods to the buyer's door and be liable for all the costs and taxes to that point, they need merely say:

DDP Purchaser's factory Nottingham (Incoterms 2000).

Export licences

Political and military events have resulted in national governments increasing control of the export of goods, services and data from their countries. It is a grave mistake to believe this control is only directed towards military goods or services or the data relating to them. Most countries have extensive lists of items requiring licences. Sometimes the reason for the inclusion of an item on a list is because of the risk that it may be used in the production of weapons or for some other purpose which may, for example, undermine public order.

Before purchasing abroad it is vital to find out if that which is to be procured is subject to the granting of a licence.

Unfortunately, if a licence is required it is not usually possible for it to be obtained prior to making the contract. The attitude of many export licensing agencies is to grant them only when the transaction is complete.

Additionally, there is always a risk, during the time between the making of the contract and delivery, that a requirement for an export licence may be introduced where none was required or that an existing licence may be withdrawn.

The risks associated with an export licence cannot be overcome completely, but a purchaser should consider the following actions:

- At the pre-contract stage find out if a licence is, or may be, necessary.

- If the would-be supplier claims no licence is required then ask that this statement be included in the contract. If this turns out to be untrue the supplier will be in breach.

- Where a licence is or may be required, place the contractual duty on the supplier to obtain and maintain it.

- Where the supplier does need to obtain a licence, then have contractual provisions entitling the purchaser to periodic written progress reports on the application included and also require the supplier to provide warnings of any factors which may result in delay in its grant.

- Provide that if delay in delivery is caused by export licensing problems then the purchaser is entitled to terminate and recover any advance payments.

Although a delay in delivery caused by export licensing difficulties may hurt a supplier as well as a purchaser it is not unknown for suppliers to slow applications down. This is likely to happen where failure to obtain the licence may amount to a defence to late delivery.

A further consideration is that there may be conditions placed on the licence by the issuing agency. One well-known restriction is that there must be no further export by the purchaser to a third country. This may raise insuperable problems for the purchaser of goods which it buys to resell abroad, either in the same form as it receives them or after processing or incorporation into other items.

Payment

The disadvantage of international trade is that obtaining money from an unwilling debtor is more difficult and expensive where the debtor chooses to hide behind its frontiers.

For this reason any deposits or other payments in advance of delivery should only be made after consideration is given to obtaining a bank guarantee or other similar document from the purchaser which allows the purchaser to obtain repayment if, for example, it exercises a right to terminate the contract.

Legal personality

It is important to be satisfied that the potential supplier is an entity recognised in its own country as having the legal capacity to enter into a valid contract. If it does not have capacity then there will be no means of enforcing the contract.

Even if it does have capacity will any judgment or arbitral award be enforceable against it? In the case of purchasing from an agency of a foreign government is it possible that enforcement in its own country may not be legally possible on the grounds of sovereign immunity or similar?

Language

In contract negotiations between parties with different mother tongues, misunderstandings and mistakes easily happen. Where negotiations are in English the foreign party may appear to comprehend better than is actually the case. Anyone speaking a foreign language tries to appear as fluent as possible. To do so they often resort to rehearsing what they wish to say just before saying it which allows a fast verbal delivery which disguises some unfamiliarity with the language. If in any doubt, try to arrange for proper translators to be on hand.

If contractual documentation or documents which have to be delivered under the contract require translation then the general rule is that the translation should be done by a translator who is translating into his or her mother tongue. Particularly where a mistranslation could compromise safety, or result in considerable damage, it is not satisfactory to use someone who has no more than a good knowledge of the language of that which is to be translated. Translators are professionals who have the skill and experience which make them more likely to recognise difficulties.

CHAPTER 20

Ethics in purchasing

Whether or not they are spelled out in his contract of employment every employee, as his employer's agent, has duties. These include:

- a duty not to make a secret profit in the course of his employment;

- a duty to safeguard his employer's property;

- a duty not to put himself into a position where his personal interest and his duty to his employer conflict, without the agreement of his employer;

- a duty to be diligent.

The first of these prohibits an agent from taking bribes whether in the form of cash, goods or services. It is also a breach of this duty to take advantage of such things as *free gifts* made by a supplier when a purchase is made.

Secret profits may be claimed by the employer from the employee. Furthermore, if a bribe has been invested and produced profit, the employer is entitled to that profit.

A recent decision of the House of Lords has made a spectacular extension in the rules relating to the recovery of secret profits. The Crown was held to be entitled to recover £90,000 in book royalties held by George Blake's publishers.

Blake had spied for the Soviet Union during the time he was employed by the British security service. He had been imprisoned but escaped and fled to Russia in 1965. Many years later he wrote his autobiography. In fact it was so many years later that by the time the book was published there was nothing in it which breached the duty of confidence Blake owed to the Crown.

The court exercised its discretion and ordered Jonathan Cape Limited to account for those royalties to the Crown. Although their lordships stressed that the facts of the case were exceptional it is a decision of the highest court and it will be interesting to see what further attempts will be made to use it.

The words *secret profits* are used to distinguish corrupt gifts from the *perks* which fall to an employee and of which the employer has knowledge. It is easy to accept and understand that a payment of money made by a would-be supplier to a member of a purchasing department is a flagrant breach of duty but other gifts are not as easy to categorise.

Most employees feel comfortable with accepting low-value items such as diaries, calendars and mouse mats. Because they feel comfortable with them they usually make no attempt to hide them from the eyes of their colleagues. Indeed, very often they use them in the course of their employment. It would be a rare employer who would object to its staff receiving such presents.

But what is the position when the gift is of a greater value – when, for example, lunch in the supplier's canteen becomes dinner at the Savoy? The short answer is that a breach of duty can only be avoided by seeking consent from a responsible and senior employee within the recipient's own organisation.

The consent must be made with a full knowledge of the facts. If the supplier's invitation is to fly to Paris and have dinner at a top restaurant, consent should be sought for this – it is not sufficient just to ask permission to be taken to dinner.

It is no answer to an action for breach of this first duty that the gift had no effect on the decision of the recipient. If there are two bidders, X and Y, to accept a gift from X is still a breach even if the recipient awards the contract to Y.

The duty to safeguard the property of the employer is a wide ranging one. It would, for example, be breached by an unauthorised disclosure by an employee of his employer's confidential information.

The duty of an employee to avoid a conflict of interest is of particular relevance to purchase staff. They are employed to buy on behalf of their employer. They cannot, without consent, place contracts to buy from themselves or from a third party over whom they have some interest or control. To do so could result in a liability to pay any profit to the employer.

The duty to be diligent means that an employer must use the skill he or she has. To refrain consciously from trying to make a good purchasing contract, whether out of laziness or for some other reason, is a breach which could have consequences for the employee. These could include a liability for damages for any loss caused to the employer.

The receipt of unauthorised gifts, in addition to being a breach of the first duty, may also be a breach of the criminal law. The law relating to corrupt gifts is largely contained in the Public Bodies Corrupt Practices Act 1889, the Prevention of Corruption Act 1906 and the Prevention of Corruption Act 1916.

The 1889 Act makes it a criminal offence for a member of a public body to accept a corrupt gift, loan, fee, reward or advantage. The donor is also guilty of a criminal offence. A public body includes local and public bodies of all descriptions.

The 1906 Act makes it a crime for an agent to receive any corrupt gift or consideration as an inducement or reward for doing or for not doing something or for favouring or disfavouring someone in relation to his employer's business. The donor is also guilty.

The 1906 Act applies to agents (which includes employees) in both the public and private sectors.

The 1916 Act tightens the screw by providing that in a prosecution under either of the other two Acts there is a presumption that the provision of any money, gift or other consideration to an employee in the public sector is presumed to be corrupt and the onus of proof is on the defendant to show there is no corruption.

There is some case law on what is meant by corruption. It is wider than dishonesty. Taking a bribe or other gift but not letting it affect a judgment is still a crime. Mere acceptance constitutes the offence.

How may corruption be prevented in the purchasing world? Over the last 15 years, companies and public bodies all over the world have created for themselves codes of conduct which contain general ethical principles, including prohibitions of both the offering of bribes and the acceptance of them. Often these codes contain guidelines as to what gifts and entertainment may or may not be accepted. It is also common to provide a *hotline* to a senior official (often the company secretary) allowing employees to report breaches of the code.

The Public Interest Disclosure Act 1998 has introduced amendments to the Employment Rights Act 1996 to protect employees who disclose malpractices in the workplace. The 1998 Act (often called 'The Whistleblowers' Charter') gives to such employees in respect of their disclosure:

- a right not to be victimised;

- a right not to be dismissed; and

- a right not to be selected for redundancy.

The scheme of the legislation is that generally, such a disclosure must be made to the worker's employer, but in certain circumstances the protection extends to disclosures made to outsiders, including the police and the media.

To have a code of conduct is admirable but just to issue one to all the staff and then to forget about it is unsatisfactory. Every purchasing area must have an active and continuous anti-corruption culture. This is easy to say but sometimes hard to achieve, although the following may assist:

- encourage all staff to seek consent before accepting hospitality from suppliers;

- encourage them to be open about offers of gifts or hospitality which are made to them;

- do not leave one person to monopolise a particular purchasing activity – make sure other people are involved and understand what it is that is being purchased;

- corruption deterrence must be consistent throughout any organisation and it is unforgivable if senior people do not lead by example.

It is of paramount importance for everyone involved in purchasing to act as a professional and to be treated as a professional.

Appendix

Butler Machine Tool Co v *Ex-Cell-O Corporation* 1979

This case illustrates *the battle of the forms* – see Chapter 3. The sequence of events was:

- On *23 May* the seller provided the buyer with a written quotation for a machine tool to be sold on the seller's standard terms of business. These included a clause which allowed the price to be varied at the time of delivery to take account of any additional costs. Delivery was stated to be 10 months from an order.

- On *27 May* the buyer replied in writing, saying:

   Please supply on terms and conditions as below and overleaf.

The buyer's terms differed from the seller's – in particular, there was no price variation clause. The buyer's order had a tear-off slip to be completed by the seller and then returned to the buyer. The slip contained these words:

Acknowledgement: Please sign and return to Ex-Cell-O. We accept your order on the terms and conditions stated therein – and undertake to deliver by [...] Date [...] Signed.

- On *5 June* the seller wrote to the buyer:

  We have pleasure in acknowledging receipt of your official order dated May 27 covering the supply of one Butler Double Plane Miller. This being delivered in accordance with our revised quotation of May 23 ... We return herewith duly completed your acknowledgement of order form.

The Court of Appeal construed the seller's letter of 5 June with its enclosed acknowledgement slip to be an acceptance of the buyer's terms. The reference to the quotation of 23 May was only to identify the machine and its price and was not an attempt by the seller to impose its standard terms on the buyer.

Accordingly, the contract was a fixed price one and the seller could not recover its excess costs. The last piece of paper of relevance in this battle of the forms was the buyer's reply of 27 May.

Dillon v *Baltic Shipping Company* 1991

This case is a good example of a party trying to introduce a term into a contract after the contract is complete and is similar to *Olley* v *Marlborough Court Hotel* – see Chapter 3.

- On *30 October 1985* the plaintiff paid a deposit for a sea cruise.

- On *9 November* she received a document headed: *Booking Form CTC Cruises*. CTC was the agent of the defendant. The document contained information about the ship and the cruise and stated:

  Contract of Carriage for travel as set out ... will be made only at the time of issuing of tickets and will be subject to the conditions and regulations printed on the tickets.

- On *6 December* the plaintiff paid the balance of her fare.

- On *24 January 1986* she received her ticket on which was printed an exemption clause limiting the defendant's liability to passengers for personal injury.

- On *16 February*, while the plaintiff was at sea, the ship struck a rock and sank. The plaintiff suffered personal injuries and nervous shock.

This was an Australian case which came before the Court of Appeal of New South Wales. The court decided that the contract was made either:

- when the ticket was issued; or

- when the plaintiff received the ticket.

In either case it was too late for the defendant to introduce this term. The court took the view that to be incorporated into the contract the clause would have had to be drawn to the plaintiff's attention in the booking form.

Griffith v *Tower Publishing Company* 1897

This case illustrates that a party is not able to assign its rights where the personality of that party is important to the other party – see Chapter 14.

Here, there was a publishing agreement between an author and a publishing company. The evidence was that the author had chosen to contract with that particular publisher as he respected the ability of the company.

The court decided that the company could not assign its rights under the contract without the author's consent. It rejected the argument that there could not be an objection as the publisher was a company rather than an individual.

The judge took the view that a company may have a reputation to maintain and that it may inspire confidence through its directors and employees. That such people might resign or be dismissed was not relevant as it would be presumed that a well-managed company would seek to employ good replacements for them.

Maritime National Fish Ltd v *Ocean Trawlers Ltd* **1935**

This case illustrates that self-induced frustration of a contract does not allow the person inducing it to rely on the doctrine of frustration. It is also an example of the inability of a party to escape liability when the frustrating event is one which is, or should have been, in that party's contemplation when the contract was made – see Chapter 15.

Here, a fishing company chartered a trawler called *St Cuthbert*, which was fitted with, and could only be operated with, an otter trawl.

At the time the parties agreed an extension of the charter of the *St Cuthbert*, the fishing company was well aware of a Canadian statute which required a licence to fish with an otter trawl. The fishing company operated five ships with otter trawls and applied for five licences.

The Canadian government made clear it would only grant three licences and the fishing company supplied the names of three of its ships which were duly licensed. The *St Cuthbert* was not among them.

The fishing company then claimed frustration but this was rejected by the Supreme Court of Nova Scotia. The case then went to the final appeal court, the Privy Council.

The Privy Council rejected the appeal on the basis that the appellant had induced the frustration – it could have nominated the *St Cuthbert* as one of the ships to be licensed but did not. Although it was not necessary for it to do so, the court also referred to the knowledge of the appellant at the time the contract was extended of the existence of the Canadian legislation.

May and Butcher v *R* 1934

This case shows the danger of leaving important gaps in a contract – see Chapter 6. It is also relevant to section 8(2) of the Sale of Goods Act 1979 which provides that where the price is not determined:

> ... the buyer must pay a reasonable price.

This contract purported to give the buyer the right to buy all government surplus tentage. The words at the centre of the litigation were:

> The Commission hereby confirm the sale to you of the whole of the old tentage which may become available ... upon the following terms:

> The price or prices to be paid ... shall be agreed upon from time to time ...

The House of Lords held that their effect rendered the transaction merely an *agreement to agree* and so not an enforceable contract.

In his judgment, Lord Buckmaster said:

> It has long been a well-recognised principle of contract law that an agreement between two parties to enter into an agreement in which some critical part of the contract matter is left undetermined is no contract at all.

Viscount Dunedin rejected the argument that section 8(2) could plug the hole in the agreement by requiring the would-be buyer to pay a reasonable price:

> The simple answer in this case is that the Sale of Goods Act provides for silence on the point and here there is no silence, because there is a provision that the two parties are to agree.

Pantland Hick v Raymond & Reid 1893

This decision of the House of Lords confirms that where a supplier's obligation is to perform a contract *within a reasonable time* the supplier will be excused any delay which was beyond its reasonable control – see Chapter 15.

Here, a cargo was shipped to London under bills of lading which did not specify the time within which it was to be unloaded. Unloading was delayed due to a strike. It was not possible to arrange alternative labour.

The court held that the contract was performed within a reasonable time even though the strike caused the unloading to take almost a month. Had there not been a strike unloading would have been completed in six days.

Simpson v *The London and North Western Railway Company* 1876

The plaintiff regularly exhibited samples of his goods at agricultural shows and made a profit by doing so. While attending a show in Bedford he contracted with the agent of the defendant for the defendant to deliver his samples to Newcastle. His purpose was to exhibit the samples at an agricultural show to be held there. The samples arrived too late and the plaintiff sued for loss of profit.

The court was of the view that the defendant's agent was aware that the plaintiff exhibited at agricultural shows and that it was his intent to do so in Newcastle. As the defendant had notice of the object for which the goods were being sent the plaintiff had a valid claim under Rule 2 of *Hadley* v *Baxendale* – see Chapter 17.

Wallis, Son & Wells v *Pratt and Haynes* 1911

This case provides useful commentary on section 11(4) of the Sale of Goods Act which results in a buyer, who has accepted goods, losing the right to reject them for breach of a condition – see Chapter 7. It is also an example of the court construing exemption clauses *contra proferentem* – see Chapter 11.

The sellers sold goods by description as *common English sainfoin* (sainfoin is used as cattle fodder). The buyers resold it as such to others by the same description. When it grew it was discovered to be an inferior variety, *giant sainfoin*, and the buyers had to compensate their customers.

When the buyers sued, the sellers attempted to rely on the following term in the contract:

> Sellers give no warranty expressed or implied as to growth, description or any other matters.

The House of Lords decided:

- there had been a breach of the condition implied by section 13 of SGA that goods shall correspond with their description;

- the combined effect of section 35 (acceptance) and section 11 was that the breach of condition 'can only be treated as a breach of warranty' (section 11(4));

- although section 11(4) said the breach had to be *treated* as a breach of warranty this did not *make* the implied term a warranty; and

- the exemption clause only attempted to exclude liability for breaches of *warranty*.

As far as the *contra proferentem* construction is concerned it is almost possible to sense the relish with which the court ruled against the seller. Lord Loreburn, the Lord Chancellor, seemed unable to resist twisting the knife:

> But if it is desired by a seller to throw the risk of any honest mistake on to the buyer, then he must use apt language, and I should have thought the clearer he tries to make the language the better.

It is not fanciful to suggest that if, at the time the contract was made, both merchants were asked what the words meant they would have said that the words were intended to exclude the seller's liability for misdescription.

Index